The Red Door Detective Club
The Mystery of the UFO

by Janet Riehecky
illustrated by Lydia Halverson

FOREST HOUSE ®

Forest House Publishing Company, Inc.
Lake Forest, Illinois

FOREST HOUSE ®

Copyright ® 1996 by Janet Riehecky
Copyright ® 1996 illustrations by Lydia Halverson
All rights reserved.
Published by Forest House Publishing Co., Inc.
P.O. Box 738
Lake Forest, Illinois 60045

Library of Congress Cataloging-in-Publication Data
Riehecky, Janet, 1953-
The mystery of the UFO / by Janet Riehecky;
illustrated by Lydia Halverson.
p. cm. – (The Red Door Detective Club : bk. 2)
Summary: When UFO sightings are reported at Sunrise Campground,
detectives Kyle and Karen and their friend Patrick are determined to investigate.
ISBN 1-56674-088-6
[1. Mystery and detective stories. 2. Unidentified flying objects – Fiction
3. Camping – Fiction.] I. Halverson, Lydia, ill. II. Title.
III. Series: Riehecky, Janet, 1953– Red Door Detective Club ; bk. 2.
PZ7.R4277Mys   1994
[Fic]--dc20   94-929
CIP
AC

Printed and bound in the United States of America.
1 2 3 4 5 6 7 8 9 R 03 02 01 00 99 98 97 96

The Red Door Detective Club

The Mystery of the UFO

Chapter 1

Kyle Lockhart sauntered out the back door of his house and headed toward the clubhouse he and his twin sister Karen had built in their back yard. It was a great clubhouse, the best one they'd ever built. They had made it with real pine boards. It was six feet tall with a flat, fiberboard roof. The walls were five feet long and there was one window in the left side wall. The door was a real door that their father had helped them with. It looked perfect sitting in the shade of a large oak tree in their back yard. But as Kyle reached the clubhouse, he let out a howl. "Karen!"

Inside the clubhouse, Karen giggled. She knew why Kyle was yelling, but she pretended to be innocent as she stuck her head out the door of their clubhouse. Kyle stood there looking outraged. He and Karen were twins, but they didn't look alike. Karen took after their dad: brown hair, dark brown eyes, and a tan complexion. Kyle normally had blond hair, blue eyes, and fair skin, like their mother, but right now his face glowed bright red.

"What's the matter, Kyle?" Karen asked, as if she were terribly concerned.

"That sign!" Kyle sputtered.

Karen stepped outside and studied the neatly-lettered sign she had just hung on the clubhouse door. It read The Red Door Detective Club.

"Did I spell something wrong?" she asked Kyle.

"You got the whole thing wrong!"

"You mean you've changed your mind about opening our own detective club?"

"You know that's not what I mean. It was bad enough when you painted our clubhouse door red — behind my back I might add. I'm not going to advertise it by calling our agency The Red Door Detective Club."

"It's a great name," Karen insisted. "It'll make us stand out from the crowd. Everybody picks names like A-1 Detective Agency or Dynamic Detectives. Our name will make people curious. They'll want to know what's behind the red door, so they'll call us."

Kyle scowled. "We could call it the Lockhart Detective Agency, after us. That's unique."

"How would Patrick feel about that? He's not a Lockhart, and he had just as much to do with finding that half million dollars and catching the crooks as we did."

For a moment Kyle smiled, remembering the thrill just two weeks before when they'd found a chest with stacks of money in a hidden room in Patrick's uncle's old house. He also remembered the terror of having one of the crooks holding a gun on him, Karen, and their friend Patrick. Patrick had gotten them out of that mess.

"OK, that wouldn't do. But there must be a better name than The Red Door Detective Club."

"Well, until you think of one, we'll just leave this here." Karen smiled sweetly and changed the subject. "Patrick called awhile ago and said he was on his way over. He said he had a surprise for us. I hope it's another mystery." She led the way into the clubhouse and Kyle followed, scowling just once more at the sign and the bright red door.

Karen and Kyle had worked hard at fixing up the inside of the clubhouse. Their mother had let them have an old piece of brown shag carpeting that had once been in their living room. She had also given them some old curtains, white with blue and green flowers. Karen and Kyle had added three camp stools, an old card table, and a box to keep their files in. They had painted the walls blue. The best decoration, though, was a framed picture of Sherlock Holmes that Kyle had found in a second hand store.

Kyle flopped onto a camp stool while Karen sprawled on her stomach on the carpet with the mystery novel she had been reading. Only a minute elapsed before they heard Patrick call as he came into the back yard. They heard him laugh and then he walked in.

Patrick was tall and skinny with short, dark hair. His looks were sort of average, but he moved with the grace of a natural athlete. He had earned a brown belt in karate and practiced constantly to improve his skill.

"Nice sign," he said, teasing Kyle.

"See," said Karen. "Patrick thinks it's a great name too."

"I didn't say that," Patrick protested with a smile. "Anyway, leave me out of it. I'll go along with whatever you two can agree on." He paused a second and then said, "Guess what?"

"Another mystery?" Karen quickly asked.

"I wish. No. But I do have good news. My dad wants to take Jonathan and me camping for a week, and he says I can invite you guys to come along." Jonathan was Patrick's cousin, even though he was almost as old as Patrick's dad. He had been gone for years, but Patrick, Karen and Kyle had found out where he was while solving **The Mystery of the Missing Money.** Jonathan had gotten into all kinds of trouble with alcohol and drugs and had even spent a year in jail, but he ended up in a twelve-step recovery group and had straightened out his life. Patrick and his dad were just getting to know him. "Jonathan's girlfriend, Melanie Anderson, will be coming too, so you won't be the only girl," Patrick added, looking at Karen.

"That sounds wonderful!" Karen exclaimed. "I'm sure our parents will let us go."

"Where will we go?" Kyle asked, just as excited.

"We haven't decided yet. Dad is going to try to get next week off to go. We can't go too far for just a week, but there are lots of good places close by."

Just then they heard someone knocking at the clubhouse door. Patrick was next to it, so he opened it. A slim, pretty, African-American girl with tiny, intricate braids and large brown eyes stuck her head in. "Hi," she said.

"Come on in, Sarah," Karen called. Sarah was one of Karen's best friends. "What have you been up to? I haven't seen you in a week."

"My family went camping over at Sunrise Campground."

"I've heard that place is a dump," Kyle said.

"Kyle! That's not very nice to say."

"That's OK, Karen. We went there because it's close and all we wanted to do was swim and hike a little. It's not the greatest place in the world, but it's not that bad. Anyway, that's why I came over. Something really weird happened while we were there. And I remembered how you guys solved that mystery a couple weeks ago."

"What happened?" Karen asked.

"You guys are going to think I'm nuts, but I'm not the only person who saw it. Lots of other people saw it too."

"Saw what?" Karen demanded.

"There were these lights. Weird lights. And they weren't on any airplane."

"What are you talking about?"

"I saw a UFO. I know it was a UFO. It couldn't have been anything else."

Karen, Kyle, and Patrick all stared at Sarah in amazement. She didn't look like she was joking around.

"What exactly did you see?" Kyle asked.

"I don't know. Some other people said they saw this round silver thing with a dome on top, but all I saw was lights. Red and white lights going around in a circle up in the sky. It was the spookiest thing I've ever seen."

"It couldn't have been a real UFO," Patrick said, but his tone was hesitant as if he wanted to believe her."

"Did you hear anything?" Kyle asked.

"I don't remember. Maybe a buzzing noise, but not anything loud or unusual. The animals in the woods were all scared away by it."

"Tell us exactly what happened," Karen ordered.

Sarah settled herself on a camp stool and leaned forward, speaking dramatically. "It was out in the woods the third night we were there. The moon was bright, so my brother and I were out looking for deer. We saw one too! Anyway, all of a sudden all the birds took off and the squirrels and stuff. And that's when I heard that buzzing sound. Billy and I looked up and we saw these lights way up above the trees. There were about two dozen red and white lights in a circle, flashing on and off. It circled over us and then took off. I only saw it that once, but other people saw it on different nights."

"It was probably just some kid's toy," said Kyle.

"No way," said Sarah emphatically. "It was way too big for that. And why would a kid be flying a toy at 10:00 at night? And the parents would have said something the next day because everybody in the campground was talking about it. I think a reporter from the paper is even going to go out there and do a story on it."

Karen, Kyle, and Patrick exchanged glances. "Are you guys thinking what I'm thinking?" Patrick asked them.

"You bet!" they exclaimed together. Kyle added, "Ask your dad if we can go camping at Sunrise Campground. We've got a mystery to solve!"

"I knew you guys would want to investigate," Sarah said with a satisfied smile.

*   *   *   *   *   *   *   *   *   *   *

Karen and Kyle easily obtained permission from their parents to go camping with Patrick and his dad, but unexpectedly, Patrick's dad proved to be a problem.

"Sunrise Campground?" Mr. Burnidge gave a bluff, hearty laugh. They were in the living room of Patrick's house, and Mr. Burnidge sat in a big, black leather recliner, shaking his head. The three detectives sat together on the couch. "Well, I guess you can't expect to find old heads on young shoulders," he said. "Don't you children know that place is the seediest dump within fifty miles of Preston? Nobody goes there who can afford anything better."

Karen clenched her teeth, biting back an angry retort. When her parents called her child, it sounded affectionate and she didn't mind. But the way Mr. Burnidge said "children" sounded terribly insulting, as if being twelve meant they were stupid.

Kyle was less sensitive to things like that. He was just concerned with convincing Mr. Burnidge that Sunrise Campground wasn't that bad.

"A friend of ours just came back from there. It's not so bad. There's a swimming pool and a river you can canoe on. And there are trees everywhere." Mr. Burnidge still looked skeptical, so Kyle continued. "The real reason we want to go there is because our friend said everybody there saw a UFO and . . ."

Kyle couldn't go on because Mr. Burnidge began to laugh and laugh. Just then Jonathan walked in the room. He was a tall, muscular man with sandy hair and a bristling mustache. "What's so funny?" he asked.

"The kids want to go to some campground that specializes in UFOs," Mr. Burnidge said, still chuckling.

"You know, I've heard some pretty convincing stories about UFOs," Jonathan said quite seriously.

Kyle sent him a grateful smile.

"Really?" said Patrick, still a little shy of his new-found cousin. "Like what?"

"Well, they've been seen by some pretty reputable people: police officers, airline pilots, priests — even former President Jimmy Carter."

Mr. Burnidge chuckled again, but as he looked at Patrick, his face softened. "Well, I guess there might be something there. After all, there's no smoke without a fire. I suppose, if all of you want to go to Sunrise Campground, we can."

"Yay!" shouted Kyle, Karen, and Patrick together.

*   *   *   *   *   *   *   *   *   *   *

Karen spent the next few days gathering everything she thought she might need for the camping trip. "Sleeping bags, flashlights, extra batteries, life jackets, swim suits, candy bars, camera, magnifying glass, books, first aid supplies, clothes and all that stuff. Kyle, what am I forgetting?"

Kyle just groaned at the mountain of supplies Karen had stacked on her bed and returned to his book. He was spending his time reading up on UFOs.

"Say Karen, did you know Sarah's description fits with lots of other UFO sightings? Red and white lights blinking in a circle are some of the most commonly reported UFOs. And usually there isn't any noise coming from them."

Despite herself Karen was sidetracked from the important issue of surviving in the wilderness. "What else does it say?" she asked.

"Well, there are some instances of hoaxes, of course. Some people claim to see weird things or take pictures of a model as a joke or to get their picture in the paper. But this book says that only covers about 5% of the reported sightings. And about 85% are mistakes, like a weather balloon or something. But that leaves 10% that are genuinely mysterious. And this book tells all kinds of really convincing stories."

"Like what?"

"Like the Exeter, New Hampshire sightings. They happened in 1965. This guy was hitchhiking home one night about two in the morning. He was cutting across a field and saw this big glowing object in the sky. It was like ninety feet wide and had red glowing lights. He thought it was chasing him, so he dove in a ditch."

"He was probably just drunk or making it up."

"No he wasn't. He went to the police and a cop went back out to the field with him. And he saw it too."

"The cop saw it?"

"That's right. And lots of other people saw it too. A woman driving a car said it chased her and lots of other people saw the lights. And nobody was ever able to figure out what it was."

"That is spooky. Were there any aliens?"

"Not in Exeter, but there are lots of sightings that did involve what might have been aliens." He thumbed through his book. "Here's one that happened in Socorro, New Mexico in 1964. A police officer was chasing a speeder and saw an explosion off on a back road. He went to investigate and saw a shiny, white, egg-shaped object in a gully, with two short figures next to it. The figures were about four feet tall and wore white coveralls. The policeman went around a ridge and couldn't see it for a while, but when he came up to it, he could see the white thing was this weird oval standing on four legs. And there was a red design on the side. The figures were gone and then when he got out of the car, there was a loud roar and the thing took off into the air. It went up about fifteen feet and just hovered there and then the noise faded to a whine and then silence and then it flew away."

"Well, that could have been short scientists working on some secret project."

"Yeah, it might have been, but how about this one." He flipped over a few more pages. "These guys were chopping trees in a National Forest in Arizona in 1975. There were seven of them and they didn't even all know each other. And anyway, on the way home they saw these strange lights and went to go see what it was. And there was this strange round object, about twenty feet wide and eight feet tall just hovering about fifteen feet off the ground. One guy — his name was Travis Walton — got out of the car to look at it and it zapped him with a beam of light. He fell down like he was unconscious and the other guys took off, they were so scared. They came back about half an hour later. They were still scared, but they felt really bad about leaving Travis. Anyway, when they found the clearing again, the object and Travis were both gone.

"The police and about fifty people looked for Travis for two days and couldn't find any trace of him. They gave up then because they figured he must be dead. The temperature was below freezing every night and they thought nobody could live out there without shelter. Then five days later Travis called his family from a phone booth twelve miles away. When they got to him, he didn't look like he'd been outside for all those days. Travis said he'd awakened on a table inside the object they'd seen. He thought it was some kind of spaceship. And there were these weird people on it. They were about five feet tall with bald heads and big eyes and white marshmallow-like skin. He said the spaceship landed in a hangar and that he saw other humans there, but when he tried to talk to them, the guys with the bald heads put something over his face and he passed out. He woke up on the road near the phone booth he called from. He thought he'd only been gone a few hours instead of five days."

"They could have made up that story."

"Maybe, but why would they? And anyway all except one of them passed lie detector tests about it."

"That really is weird."

"There are all kinds of stories like that in these books. And a lot of them really sound like they happened."

"Well, I can't wait to get to Sunrise Campground and find out about the UFO there. But we're not going to get there at all if you don't help me pack!" Karen threw a pillow at Kyle. He laughed and ducked and threw one back.

Chapter 2

Karen was completely packed two days before she needed to be. Kyle shook his head in amazement at the quantity of things she seemed to feel were absolutely necessary for the trip. "It's a good thing Mr. Burnidge has a van," he told her. Karen laughed and predicted he'd be begging her for supplies when they were miles and miles away from civilization.

The day to leave was a perfect summer day — ninety degrees with just a few pure white clouds in the sky. Mr. Burnidge actually seemed to be pleased at the mound of luggage Karen was bringing. He patted her on the shoulder and told her it was better to be safe than sorry. Jonathan introduced the twins to his girlfriend, Melanie Anderson. She was a tall woman in her early thirties with very curly short black hair. Kyle thought she was pretty and Karen liked the way her eyes lit up when she smiled.

The campground was just a short distance beyond the city limits of Preston. There were two forest preserves in the area and several large farms. Jonathan was the first to spot the sign which said "Sunrise Campground." Everyone cheered, but it was a half-hearted cheer. The old, weather-beaten sign hung crooked and hadn't been painted in twenty years. Several letters could no longer be read, so it actually said "Sun is   Ca   round."

Mr. Burnidge followed a dirt road to a dilapidated building with the word "Office" stenciled on one of the doors. The building had obviously not been painted since the last time the sign had been. The office screen door hung from a single hinge and the screens were all ripped allowing insects easy entrance. Not that that mattered, seeing there were neither screens nor glass in the office windows. The rest of the building appeared to be a general store, stocking the types of supplies campers were most likely to need. It appeared to be better maintained than the office, but Karen was glad they had brought their own supplies.

An older man who hadn't shaved in several days shuffled out of the office and approached the car. Mr. Burnidge stepped out of the car, stretching his arms and legs. "Reservation for Burnidge," he said to the man.

"That'll be twenty dollars a night," the old man said, scratching his belly, not even bothering to check his records.

Mr. Burnidge scowled at the fee, which was twice what he had expected, but he didn't say anything. He wrinkled his nose at the odor coming from the man and paid for six nights. "Is there any electrical hookup?" he asked.

"What'd ya come camping for?" the old man asked scornfully. "Ta live like ya was in a hotel?" He shuffled back into the office and returned a few minutes later, handing them a greasy ticket for campsite 27. "Jest go down around the curve there and follow them numbers." Then he turned and wandered back into the office, dismissing them.

Mr. Burnidge stood for a moment as if deciding whether to go after the man or not, but he looked at his son and thought better of it. He got back in the car without saying anything and headed slowly down the dirt road, carefully avoiding potholes.

As they rounded the curve, the noise of water splashing and people laughing drifted in the window. "Sounds like everyone at the pool is having fun," Patrick said tentatively, stealing a look at his father. Mr. Burnidge tried to smile at him, but the corners of his mouth refused to turn up.

As they drove down the winding road, they noticed that only about half the campsites were occupied. "I'm surprised even this many people would deliberately come here," Mr. Burnidge muttered.

Karen held her breath as they passed number 26 and rounded a bend. Then she saw campsite 27 and gasped. It was beautiful. It was in a small clearing surrounded by beautiful oak and maple trees. Whoever had camped there last had left the clearing immaculate. There wasn't the tiniest scrap of litter, and the picnic table, though needing paint, was clean and neat. Even the grill wasn't too bad and there was a rock-lined pit for a campfire.

Everyone tumbled out of the car, their enthusiasm stronger than it might have been if their expectations hadn't been so low. Mr. Burnidge, Jonathan, and Kyle set up a big dome tent for the men, while Patrick helped Melanie and Karen set up a slightly smaller trail tent for the two women. Kyle warned Melanie not to let Karen have any say in how their tent looked.

"If you don't watch her, she's likely to paint the whole thing red," he teased.

"But I like red," Melanie said, winking at Karen. She obviously had heard the whole story about the club house.

"I should have known," Kyle muttered. "Women always stick together." He returned to helping Jonathan unload supplies.

Setting everything up took about half an hour. After they finished, Karen looked around in satisfaction. It really was a beautiful place, though now that she thought about it, a little red really would brighten up all this green. But before she could take that idea any farther, Patrick yelled, "Last one in the pool has to wash the dishes tonight!" and everyone scrambled to get into their swimsuits.

The three detectives raced down the path toward the center of the campground, where they'd heard the noise from the pool as they drove in. Mr. Burnidge, Jonathan, and Melanie strolled along after. A few minutes brought them to a fenced-in area containing a large pool and two locker rooms. The pool was obviously old and somewhat run-down, but the grounds around it were fairly clean and neat. The locker rooms needed paint, but they didn't smell any worse than the locker rooms at the YMCA back in Preston.

Patrick and Kyle were the first ones out of the locker rooms. They raced toward the pool, each trying to be the first one in. Kyle took a short lead and glanced back over his shoulder at Patrick. Just as he did, a stocky young man about sixteen years old swerved into Kyle's path. CRASH! They collided and both were knocked to the ground.

"Gosh, I'm sorry," Kyle said, scrambling to his feet. He reached down to help the older boy up.

The young man ignored Kyle's hand and jumped to his feet. "What do you think you're doing, jerk! Why don't you watch where you're going!"

Kyle clenched his teeth, but he knew he'd been in the wrong. "I said I'm sorry. We were just having a race." From the corner of his eye he watched Patrick, who had run past as soon as he saw Kyle was all right. Patrick waved and jumped in the water.

The young man didn't respond to Kyle's apology. He just scowled and headed toward the locker room, limping slightly.

Karen had seen the whole thing and she hurried over to Kyle. "Are you all right?" she asked.

"Yeah. I'm sorry I ran into that guy, but he was really rude about it."

"Well, don't worry about it. Come on. Let's jump in."

The water was cool, but it felt good under the hot

sun. There were about a dozen other campers in the pool, but the pool was big enough that Kyle, Karen, and Patrick could have races and play water tag without disturbing anyone else. Jonathan and Melanie joined in some of the games, though they weren't as good swimmers as the three detectives. Mr. Burnidge even joined one race, surprising everyone by winning.

They swam and played for a long time, but finally Karen decided she felt like just relaxing in the sun. She called to Kyle and Patrick as she got out of the pool and they waved back, continuing their game.

Karen walked over to a cement area near the fence where she'd left her towel. Two girls a little older than she sat nearby talking. Karen gave them a friendly smile and they smiled back. As Karen began smoothing sun block on her arms, they came over.

"Hi," the first girl said. "My name is Diane and this is my sister, Barbara." Both girls were red-heads, Diane's a beautiful auburn and Barbara's just slightly darker. Barbara was taller than Diane, but, looking at their faces, it was easy to see they were sisters. Both had the same expressive green eyes.

Karen introduced herself and explained about Kyle and Patrick. The two sisters said they were there with their parents and then sat down, eager to talk.

"Have you seen the UFO?" Barbara asked.

"No. We just got here today. But I heard about it from a friend of mine who was here last week."

"We saw it just last night. Almost everyone in the campground has seen it," Diane explained eagerly.

"Tell me all about it!"

"We were hiking over there." Diane pointed to the woods north of the swimming pool, the same direction as Karen's campsite. "The sun had been down for a while, so it must have been around ten o'clock. We were pretty deep in the woods and there wasn't anybody else around. We found this clearing and so we sat down for a while just to watch the stars."

Barbara interrupted. "We were looking for the UFO," she said, darting a glance at her sister. "These two boys we met yesterday had seen it out there a couple days ago."

"Well, anyway, we sat there awhile looking up at the stars when suddenly we heard this buzzing noise."

"It sounded like my dad's electric razor, only louder," Barbara added.

"Then there were these lights, red and white in a circle. And I saw a silver dome on top the spaceship."

"I didn't see the dome," said Barbara, "But the lights went on and off and on and off. It was really spooky."

"It flew right over us as if it could see us, then it flew away." Diane gave a shiver and her eyes glowed. It might have been spooky to Barbara, but it was clear Diane had loved every minute of the encounter.

"Wow," said Karen. "What do you think it was?"

"I don't have any idea," Barbara started to say, but Diane interrupted.

"I'm sure it was an alien spaceship. What else could it have been?"

"You guys are sure it wasn't just some kid's toy?"

"Absolutely," Diane affirmed. "It was way too big."

"How big was it?"

Barbara wrinkled her forehead as if picturing the UFO again in her memory. "I'd say it was fifteen or twenty feet across. Wouldn't you, Diane?"

"At least. Though it was hard to tell because it was way up in the sky."

"How high up was it?"

Again Barbara hesitated. "It was hard to tell. About as high as some helicopters I've seen — where you can tell it's a helicopter, but it's still pretty high up in the air."

Diane nodded agreement. "We thought about going and looking for it again tonight, but it usually only shows up every couple days. At least that's what everybody says. And we have to go home tomorrow." She sighed deeply.

"I sure would like to see it," Karen said.

Diane smiled brightly. "We could show you where the clearing is. It wouldn't hurt to look tonight. It might show up — and it's a fun hike anyway."

Diane and Barbara agreed that Kyle and Patrick could come too. They arranged to come to Karen's campsite at nine that night and show them the way.

*   *   *   *   *   *   *   *   *   *   *

Dinner that night was great. Jonathan started a fire in the grill and cooked hamburgers and hot dogs, while Melanie warmed a can of baked beans. Karen and Kyle had brought some of their mother's best potato salad. Patrick had fixed carrot sticks and celery stuffed with cream cheese. Mr. Burnidge had thought ahead and set out a big jar with water and tea bags for sun tea. They all sat at the picnic table and ate every last thing.

"Mmm!" said Karen with a contented sigh. "How come everything always tastes better if you eat it outdoors?"

"It probably has something to do with fresh air and exercise increasing your appetite," Kyle said seriously. Karen rolled her eyes at him.

Patrick teased Kyle that he had to wash the dishes, seeing he'd lost the race, but there weren't very many — just the bowl from the potato salad and the tongs and flipper Jonathan had used for the meat. They'd used paper plates and cups for everything else.

Kyle didn't mind. He hiked down the road to the pump. It, like everything else in the campground, needed paint, but the handle only creaked a little bit as Kyle pumped it up and down. The water rushed out and filled the bowl. It made Kyle feel like a pioneer to have to pump his own water. His mother would have objected to his using cold water to wash dishes, but she wasn't there. He added a little dish soap and scrubbed Jonathan's cooking utensils. Everyone else had already tossed their paper plates and cups into the fire pit where Jonathan had started a fire, so all he had to do was pack his things away in the back of the van.

As Kyle returned to the campfire, Jonathan announced that he had a surprise. From a box in the back of the van he produced marshmallows, chocolate bars, and graham crackers. "Can I interest anyone in s'mores?" he asked with a knowing grin.

"Yahoo!" shouted Kyle. He liked s'mores even better than peanut butter and bologna.

Jonathan asked Karen, Kyle, and Patrick to add

some sticks to the paper in the firepit for a campfire. In no time at all he had a bright blaze going. Kyle was always very patient roasting his marshmallow. He held it above the flames, turning it carefully, until it was a golden brown. Karen tried to do that, but before too long she grew impatient. She thrust the marshmallow into the fire, let it catch and burn for a few seconds, and then blew the flame out. The inside was a delicious goo, and the black outside wasn't so bad.

Then Jonathan surprised them again. He pulled a guitar out of the back of the van and began playing "Michael, Row the Boat Ashore." Everyone — even Mr. Burnidge — joined in singing. They roasted more marshmallows and sang camp songs for an hour. Karen was having so much fun she was almost disappointed when Diane and Barbara came by. Still the chance to see a real UFO was not to be missed.

Mr. Burnidge had given them permission to go provided they all stayed together and were back by 10:30. The three detectives grabbed flashlights and cameras and Karen grabbed an old quilt she'd brought along. Then they all followed Diane and Barbara into the woods.

*　*　*　*　*　*　*　*　*　*　*

Karen felt a tingle of anticipation course up her spine. She'd been so excited she hadn't even teased Kyle when he realized he hadn't brought a flashlight and had to ask her for one. Of course, she'd packed an extra.

Their flashlights illuminated a narrow path. It was only about a foot wide, but the ground had been packed solid by many tramping feet, and no grass grew on it. There were some wild flowers near the edge of the path where the sun reached during the day — goldenrod, Queen Anne's lace, and even some delicate white blossoms of Wild Morning Glory. Some sumac leaves were just turning bright red. They looked beautiful, but Karen knew better than to get near them. She didn't want this trip spoiled by a rash. As they traveled deeper into the woods, she studied the sky, hoping to see something weird, but all she could see through the tree leaves were small patches of sky and a few scattered stars. After she tripped on a tree root, while gazing skyward, she decided she'd better just concentrate on getting to the clearing.

It took only about fifteen minutes for them to reach the small clearing Diane and Barbara had found the night before. There didn't seem to be any reason for the trees to abruptly thin out, but suddenly there was a clear area about twenty feet in diameter. Karen caught her breath as she stepped into the clearing and looked up. Even if they didn't see a UFO, it was worth the hike to see that night sky. Hundreds, probably thousands of stars sparkled brilliantly against the dense blackness. "Why do the stars always seem so much brighter in the country than in the city?" she asked in a whisper. Somehow, in that setting, it seemed wrong to talk in a normal tone of voice.

"In the city there are always some sort of lights around you. It needs to be completely dark for them to sparkle like this," Kyle responded. Karen scowled at him — not because he always seemed to know things like that, but because his prosaic tone of voice destroyed the magical mood she had felt.

No one else seemed to react to the sky the same way Karen did either. Diane giggled and said, "Look way over there." She pointed to a glimmer of light further north. "That's a farmhouse. That land borders the campground. Yesterday we explored over that way and found a barbed wire fence where the woods end."

Everyone looked and then drifted aimlessly around the clearing, studying the area and wondering what to do next. Karen could hear the rushing sound of the water in the river. Apparently it wasn't too far away.

"Last night we saw the UFO only about five minutes after we got here," Barbara said. "But there's no telling when it might show up tonight — or even if it'll show up at all."

"We can wait half an hour," Patrick said shining his flashlight on his watch, "and still be back in plenty of time. Why don't we tell some ghost stories while we wait?"

Everyone loved that idea. Karen spread the quilt she'd brought on the ground and they all crashed, jostling each other for room. Kyle jabbed Patrick in the ribs, demanding more space. Patrick jabbed him back, but moved over. Finally everyone settled down comfortably.

"I'll start," said Patrick. "Once," he began in a low, ominous voice, "there was this creepy old house way out in the country. A large family had lived there, but suddenly one night everyone in the family died. There wasn't a single mark on any of the bodies, so people said it must have been ghosts and no one would buy the house or even go in it. For years the house stood empty. Then one day this boy named Kyle," he paused dramatically and Karen giggled, "was invited to join the Secret Society of Super Scientific Spies — SSSSS for short — and his initiation required him to spend the night in that house. Kyle said that of course he wasn't scared — he'd read several books about ghosts and knew just how to talk to them. So he took some food and water and a sleeping bag and went in the house just at sunset. During the night there were loud wailings and strange groans from the house. The SSSSS members waited, wondering what was happening, but none of them was brave enough to go in to see. Morning finally came and Kyle walked out of the house. He looked perfectly fine." Here Patrick paused and looked at each person in the group. "But when he opened his mouth, he couldn't speak. And for the rest of his life, he never spoke again."

Karen, Diane, and Barbara rolled on the quilt laughing, but Kyle demanded, "What happened to me?"

"Nobody knows," Patrick replied in an eerie tone of voice. "I guess you talked too much to the ghosts."

"Humph," said Kyle.

Diane volunteered to tell the next story. As she began, Karen became aware that there was a soft, buzzing noise coming from beyond the trees. At first she ignored it, but as it grew louder, she suddenly realized what that noise might mean. Everyone seemed to realize the same thing, all at once. All of them leaped to their feet and stared up, searching the sky. Karen's heart pounded, and she suddenly thought of her camera. She bent down and grabbed it from the spot on the quilt where she'd left it. As she straightened back up, the

clearing was lit by red and white lights.

"Wow!" she breathed and everyone stared up dumbfounded. Silhouetted against the black sky was a circle of red and white lights seemingly on the underside of a round vehicle. The lights flickered on and off as the vehicle sped over the trees just north of the clearing. Karen had frozen for a moment, but then she began snapping pictures, as many as she could take. Kyle and Patrick were doing the same thing. Then, as suddenly as it had appeared, it was gone, blocked from view by the trees at the edge of the clearing.

For a moment everyone stayed completely still, staring at the spot where the UFO had disappeared. Then Diane giggled and soon everyone was laughing and laughing.

"That was incredible," gasped Patrick, trying to control his laughter. "I've never seen anything like that in my life."

"Unbelievable!" Kyle agreed. Then everyone began to talk at once, describing what they'd seen and asking if the others had seen it too.

No one had been able to see much of the craft at all, but there was no mistaking that circle of lights. Kyle was the most objective about it.

"You know," he said. "I don't think it's as big as everyone said. I think that's just an illusion. The lights are small, like Christmas tree lights, and that makes you think it's higher in the air than it is and that it's bigger than it really is."

"But it had to be at least ten feet in diameter," Karen argued.

"Maybe," Kyle replied, "but it sure wasn't fifteen or twenty."

"Well, even a ten-foot UFO is more UFO than I've ever seen before," Karen said, slightly annoyed with Kyle's analysis.

Kyle grinned at her. "Me either," he said.

No one seemed able to settle back comfortably on the quilt, and ghost stories seemed uninteresting compared to a real UFO. Diane and Barbara complained that they were leaving the next day and wouldn't get to see it again. Everyone stared up at the sky, searching every inch. But the UFO never came back.

Finally Patrick said it was time to go back to the campsite. The three detectives said good-bye to Diane and Barbara. Then with one last look over their shoulders, they hurried back down the path, eager to tell Patrick's dad and Jonathan and Melanie what they had seen.

Chapter 3

Karen spent a restless night. First there was loud rock music coming from another campsite. It wouldn't have been so bad if she could have actually heard the music, but all she could hear was the bass. Thrumm. Thrumm. Thrumm. And sometimes, for variation: DUM-DUM-DA-DUM. It didn't seem to bother Melanie. She was curled in her sleeping bag, snoring gently in time to the music. Karen sighed and tried to get comfortable. The music finally stopped, but then there seemed to be a rock poking through her air mattress, quilt, and down sleeping bag.

"I wonder if this is a test, like in that old fairy tale," she said out loud, as she wriggled about trying to find some spot to lay where she couldn't feel the rock. "But I never claimed to be a real princess, and that rock is a lot bigger than a pea."

She twisted and turned and eventually dropped off. But then she dreamed. She dreamed that aliens were invading the earth and the only way she could stop them was by painting every door in town red. But Kyle owned the paint store, and he wouldn't let her have any red paint. When she tried to tell him about the aliens, he didn't believe her. Even when red and white lights appeared and began flashing on and off in the sky outside the store, he claimed the lights were just from the store across the street which was having a sale, and he still wouldn't let her have any paint. So, Karen ran outside and began coloring all the doors with crayons. But it was too late. The sky was full of spaceships. Karen screamed and woke herself up.

Melanie appeared to be still asleep, but Karen could see a faint, grey light outside the tent. "I do not want to go back to sleep," she said out loud, and she struggled out of her sleeping bag. She made her way to the outhouse, wondering again if a real UFO made up for not having flush toilets.

When she returned to the campsite, Patrick and Kyle were up.

Kyle didn't even say, "Good morning," or suggest breakfast. He was full of enthusiastic plans. "Let's go back to the clearing now that it's daylight and see if we can find any evidence from the UFO," he said eagerly.

"I'm not going anywhere on an empty stomach," Karen announced, but Kyle and Patrick ignored her.

"What kind of evidence?" Patrick asked.

"Most likely burn marks. But maybe the UFO left a piece of itself behind. Like if it brushed against the trees, an antenna or something might have broken off. And we can hike in the direction that it went and see if there's any trace of its passage. Then tonight we can go back and see if it appears again."

"If you had let me have some red paint last night, we wouldn't have to go chasing aliens today, and then we could enjoy a nice leisurely breakfast," Karen interjected.

This got Kyle's attention, but he merely looked at her as if she'd grown a set of antennas and continued to make plans with Patrick. Karen sighed. The only way to get Kyle to think about food was to mention the word "bologna."

Jonathan stumbled out of the big tent, yawning and stretching. "I'd like to go with you tonight," he said. "I'd like to see that thing for myself."

Patrick grinned at his cousin. "That'd be great," he said. "Do you think it'll show up three nights in a row? Barbara and Diane said it was there night before last, too."

Karen realized that nobody else was interested in food, so she rummaged about in the cooler, finding milk and orange juice. Then she located bowls and a box of Cheerios — her visions of bacon and eggs cooked in the outdoors fading away. Kyle, Patrick, and Jonathan absentmindedly accepted bowls from her and continued to speculate about the UFO until Melanie and Mr. Burnidge joined them.

"I was planning to try the fishing today," Mr. Burnidge said. "Wouldn't you kids like to join me?"

Karen noticed that Patrick looked torn between wanting to spend time with his father and wanting to investigate the UFO, so she suggested, "How about fishing this afternoon and all of us hiking this morning?"

Mr. Burnidge glanced down at his brightly-polished leather shoes. "Well, I'm not sure about walking too far. I tell you what. I've got some paperwork I have to finish up. You take your hike and come back for lunch and then we'll go fishing. How's that?"

Everyone agreed, though Jonathan and Melanie decided to go swimming instead of hiking with Patrick, Kyle, and Karen. Jonathan then suggested he and Melanie take the film from all three cameras to the general store and see if they could send it out to be developed right away.

"Though what right away might mean to that manager, I don't even want to know," Jonathan said, shaking his head. "But I really would like to see what a UFO looks like on film." The three detectives agreed, then they hurriedly pitched in to clean up the breakfast things. They had a UFO to find!

* * * * * * * * * * *

Sunlight filtered through the leaves on the trees, making the woods bright and inviting instead of spooky. Karen followed Kyle and Patrick as they strolled along down the narrow, winding path. Now that her stomach was full, she was more excited about investigating what they'd seen the night before. What if the UFO really was an alien spaceship? Finding it would be even better than finding half a million dollars. Of course she wasn't really sure what she should say to an alien.

"Take me to your leader," she murmured aloud. That didn't sound very original. "How about, 'Please don't eat me?' That's at least practical." She remembered a picture from one of Kyle's books showing a short, bald creature with pasty-white skin. "Maybe they'd be grateful if I told them about suntan lotion," she speculated.

It didn't take long for the three detectives to find their way back to the clearing. The trees thinned out and there was an open, circular area about twenty feet wide. Long, thick grass covered most of the clearing, though a few brown spots showed either people or animals had spent some time there. Kyle suggested they spend some time searching it, just in case.

"There's probably nothing here," he explained, "but we need to check everything out. I'm sure they can see this clearing from the sky, so the UFO might have landed here."

It took more time than they expected to comb the area. The tangled grass hid old pop cans and various other bits of litter, some of it extremely disgusting. None of the garbage seemed otherworldly though, so eventually Kyle suggested they move on.

Everyone agreed the UFO had flown off over the northern section of trees, so they pushed through the undergrowth, following its path. It was difficult to get through. The trees were spaced far enough apart that bushes and weeds were a problem. Patrick's shirt caught on a thorn bush and ripped, and Karen kept tripping over twisted weeds. When Kyle finally found a path going sort of in the right direction, they all breathed a sigh of relief. The path wound through the trees, leading eventually to a barbed-wire fence, separating the woods from a field planted with corn.

"I remember," Karen said, "Diane told us about this. She said there was a farm over this way. Look, there's a farmhouse." The two boys stared across the field in the direction Karen was pointing. Sure enough, there was a large yellow farmhouse and a barn at the far end of the field.

"I wonder if the people that live there have seen the UFO," Kyle said. He studied the house. "Their house is right in the path where the ship was headed last night." He paused a moment as if making up his mind. Then he spoke firmly, "Let's go ask them."

"Do you think we should?" Patrick asked. "People who put up barbed-wire fences usually don't like strangers on their property."

"We're not going to hurt anything. Just ask a few questions."

Patrick and Karen shrugged their shoulders and agreed. They used some dead branches to hold the wire apart and climbed through.

They had to walk around the edge of the cornfield because the rows of corn were too close together to walk through easily. Still it was much easier going than it had been hiking through the woods. The sun beat down on them and Karen noticed that the tips of Kyle's ears were turning red. He hated that Karen tanned easily and all he ever did was burn, so Karen didn't tease him. She did suggest that he get some sunscreen on them as soon as they got back to the campsite. Kyle didn't seem to appreciate her concern, though. He just scowled and changed the subject.

"If these people haven't seen the UFO, we'll have to assume it changed course after it flew out of our sight. That means it must have gone east, because we'd have seen it if it flew south or west."

It took about fifteen minutes to walk around the field and reach the farmyard. The house was big, but sadly in need of a fresh coat of paint. The barn looked as if it had never been painted at all. Karen wrinkled her nose at the odor coming from it. "Cows," she said with a grimace.

Still there were signs someone tried to care for the place. Sunflowers grew by the side of the house and pretty blue and white curtains billowed at the windows. Three big apple trees graced a front lawn that had been recently mowed. The detectives didn't see any people as they approached, but chickens in a coop near the barn scurried about eating corn which appeared to have been recently scattered about for them.

Kyle called out a loud, "Hello," and they heard a

noise from the barn. A big, black dog bounded out of the barn, heading toward them. Kyle smiled and held out his hand. He loved all kinds of dogs. But this one wasn't wagging its tail. As it sprang toward them, it growled deep in its throat. It apparently did not love all kinds of people.

"Run!" Patrick yelled.

All three spun around and ran for the apple trees they had just passed in the front yard. Karen and Patrick reached them first. Each grabbed a low branch and swung up. Kyle, however, had hesitated too long. As he reached the closest tree and started to pull himself up, the dog caught up and sank its teeth into Kyle's foot. Kyle howled and hung in the air with the dog growling and pulling on his shoe. Kyle shook his foot violently, but the dog wouldn't let go. Kyle tugged fiercely and with a jerk his foot came free, leaving the dog with his shoe.

The animal seemed content with its prize. It lay under the tree chewing the shoe ferociously, a low growl still vibrating its throat.

"Are you all right, Kyle?" Karen gasped when she could catch her breath.

"Yeah," Kyle answered, shakily. "All he got was my shoe."

"What do we do now?" Patrick asked.

"I know," Karen said. "Help!" she yelled.

All three chorused together, "Help!" The dog

looked up at them, dropped the shoe, and began barking.

A woman with streaks of grey in her hair stuck her head out a window on the second floor of the farmhouse. "Hush up, Beetlejuice," she yelled. Then she noticed the three detectives up in the tree. "What in tarnation? I'll be right down."

To the three detectives, stuck in the tree, guarded by a vicious dog, it seemed to take an hour for the woman to reach the front yard. And she didn't seem overly concerned once she did reach it.

"Well, you're too young to be salesmen," she said staring up at them. "Unless you're peddling candy and wrapping paper for some band or something." She was an older woman, dressed in a faded blue cotton dress, her hair cut short and curling around her face. "What are you doing on my property?" she demanded.

"We came from the campground," Karen explained. "We wanted to ask you some questions about the UFO."

"Humph!" the woman replied. "If you came from the campground, that means you came through my fence. Don't kids nowadays know that fences are there for a reason?"

"We're sorry," Patrick said. "We didn't mean any harm. Could you hold onto your dog, so we can get down?"

The woman appeared reluctant to do so, but she did grasp Beetlejuice by the collar and tell him to sit. Karen, Kyle, and Patrick slid down the tree trunk. The dog growled, but did not move toward them. Kyle retrieved his shoe from the spot where the dog had left it. It now had several holes in it, but he stuck it on his foot anyway.

"We're really sorry to disturb you," Karen said, brushing bits of bark off her shorts and top. "We saw a UFO last night over at the campground, and it headed in this direction. We thought you might have seen it land."

"UFOs." The woman sounded disgusted. "You got nothing better to do than chase after lights in the sky? Just what you gonna do if you meet up with an alien? Ask if it plays basketball? Humph!"

"Did you see any lights last night?" Kyle persisted.

"Yeah, I've seen lights lots of times. Red and white they are, but I don't pay them any mind."

"Did you see where they went? Did you see it land?" Karen asked, her voice squeaking with excitement.

"They stay over by the woods near the river." The woman gestured back the way they had come, only more to the east of the spot where they had gone through the fence. "I couldn't tell if it landed or not. I didn't care."

"How many times have you seen them?" Patrick

asked.

"I really don't know," said the woman, sounding aggravated. "Maybe half a dozen. Who cares? I got more important things to worry about."

"Well, that's at least more than we knew before," Kyle said, his enthusiasm undimmed. "That is, uh, thanks."

"Humph!" said the woman again. She turned to go back to her house, muttering as she did, "Kids need more work to do. That'd keep them out of trouble." She grasped Beetlejuice by the collar and told him to come along.

"We won't bother you again," Patrick called to her back. "Thank you."

The woman didn't bother to turn around or reply. So the three detectives returned the way they had come, the sound of Beetlejuice barking spurring them on.

Chapter 4

It was nearly lunchtime by the time the three detectives climbed back over the fence into the campground woods. Kyle wanted to investigate the area where the woman had said she'd seen the UFO go, but reluctantly agreed there wasn't time right then. They retraced their path through the woods and arrived at the campsite just as Jonathan was starting a fire in the grill.

Kyle missed his usual bologna and something sandwich, but he admitted that Jonathan's cheeseburgers were almost as good. The three detectives told Mr. Burnidge, Jonathan, and Melanie about the farm woman who had given them a general direction to search in for the UFO. Somehow, though, they never mentioned being treed by Beetlejuice. Kyle kept the shoe with the holes in it out of sight.

Surprisingly, Jonathan reported that he had been able to send the film out to be developed. It would be ready in two days time. "We can't wait to see what you got on film," Melanie said with a smile.

As they were finishing the chocolate cupcakes Mr. Burnidge had brought for dessert, a pretty, blonde woman in her late twenties approached their campsite, accompanied by the young man Kyle had collided with at the pool the day before. The woman looked out of place in a campground, as she wore a blue linen suit and high heels. She carried a white leather purse and a small spiral notebook.

"These are the kids," the young man announced to the woman as they entered the campsite. He stopped short several feet away from the group and let the woman go past him, then leaned against a tree with his arms folded.

Kyle started to get to his feet, but Mr. Burnidge waved him down. "What's the problem?" he asked.

"No problem," the woman said quickly. "My

name is Darlene Patterson. I'm a reporter for the Preston Daily News. I'm doing a story on the UFO and two girls, Diane and Barbara O'Neill, told me your kids were with them when they saw it last night. I'd just like them to tell me what they saw."

Mr. Burnidge and the others relaxed. "Sure," Mr. Burnidge said. "Come have a seat." He gestured to a lawn chair near the picnic table.

"I got to go back now," the young man said abruptly. "If you want to talk to me later, you know where to find me." He stalked away as if disgusted with the whole world.

"Who is that kid?" Kyle asked Ms. Patterson, as she sat down in the lawn chair and took out a pen out of her purse.

"Kevin Turner? Oh, he's the manager's son. He's seen the UFO, too, and I guess he thought he was the only person that ought to be interviewed. Anyway, do you mind telling me about the UFO?"

"No!" exclaimed Karen. "It was great!" The others laughed and agreed to answer Ms. Patterson's questions.

"Well, first I need everyone's names." Each person gave her their full name and she wrote them all down, carefully checking the spelling. Then she asked, "Now, who exactly saw the UFO?"

"We did!" said Karen, pointing to herself, Kyle and Patrick.

"So it was just the kids, none of you were with them?" Ms. Patterson asked, making a note and turning to Mr. Burnidge, Jonathan, and Melanie.

"No, we stayed here," Mr. Burnidge replied.

Jonathan added, "But I intend to go with the next time. I want to see the thing." Melanie laughed and agreed.

Ms. Patterson smiled and turned to the three detectives. "Would you each tell me what you saw last night?" she asked.

"It really was a UFO," Karen said excitedly. "We were in a clearing up through there." She pointed to the trees north of their campsite. "I guess it was about ten o'clock when we heard a buzzing sound and then this thing flew over us. It was round, but I couldn't tell what it looked like. There were about two dozen white and red lights on the bottom of it, and they kept flickering on and off."

Ms. Patterson made some notes, then she turned to Patrick. "Is that how you saw it?"

Patrick thought for a moment. "Yes," he said slowly. "I don't think I can add anything to that."

"How about you?" she said to Kyle.

"I don't think it's as big as people keep saying," Kyle said. "Diane and Barbara said it was fifteen or twenty feet across, but I thought it was more like ten."

"That would make it kind of small for anyone to

be on board," Ms. Patterson said thoughtfully. She made another note in her notebook.

"Do you think it's really a spaceship?" Karen asked eagerly.

"Some of the people I've talked to think it is," Ms. Patterson answered, with a smile. "But a good reporter doesn't make up her mind until she has all the facts. Did you smell anything when it flew over?"

The three detectives looked at each other and frowned in concentration. "I can't really remember smelling anything," said Patrick. "I don't think I did. If there had been an unusual odor, I probably would have remembered."

"How about the animals in the woods? Did they react to the UFO?"

"They ran away," Kyle said. "I heard several animals running through the bushes and stuff. Although I think some of them were chased away just by us coming through the woods."

"Did any of you feel anything, like a sudden wind, or a change in the air pressure, or electricity in the air, or maybe heat?"

Again all three had to stop and think. Then they shook their heads no.

"And how about the craft itself. Did you see any other details or even a reflection that might indicate it was made of metal?"

Again they all shook their heads no. "It all happened so fast," Karen explained to Ms. Patterson. "And we were really excited. We didn't stop to notice everything."

Kyle hung his head. "Yeah," he said. "Some detectives we are."

Ms. Patterson looked startled and looked again at the names she had written down. "You're those kids that caught those computer chip smugglers a few weeks ago, aren't you?"

"That's us," said Karen, shooting a mischievous glance at Kyle. "We started The Red Door Detective Club."

"The Red Door Detective Club," she said, busily writing. "This could make a nice sidebar for my story. Why Red Door?"

Kyle opened his mouth to protest, but Karen talked over him, explaining about their clubhouse, which she elevated to a real detective office.

"And so after our friend told us about the UFO, we wanted to investigate, but we haven't gotten very far yet. Still we've only been here one day and we not only saw it, we got some great pictures of it."

"Pictures?" Ms. Patterson inquired eagerly.

"All three of us had cameras and we took a bunch of pictures. Some of them have to come out."

"Oh, you don't have them developed yet. I

thought . . . I'd be happy to take the film to town and get it developed for you — though I'd claim first right to see them for my fee." Ms. Patterson added the last in a voice that was only half teasing.

"We've already sent them out," Kyle explained apologetically. "The general store by the office can do that. They should be back day after tomorrow."

"Could I come back then and see them?" Ms. Patterson asked.

"Of course," all three detectives replied. Then Karen asked, "If you use one of our pictures in the newspaper, do we get paid for it?"

Ms. Patterson laughed. "Well, sometimes, but not usually." She looked back through her notes. "I think I can make a front page story out of this," she said with satisfaction. "I only hope my editor agrees."

"Has anybody else that you've talked to told you anything different about the UFO?" Kyle asked.

"Not really," Ms. Patterson replied. "Everyone's description is just about the same as yours. Nobody's really noticed anything unusual about the UFO." She laughed. "That is, of course, more unusual than strange lights in the sky." She pulled a business card out of her purse. "Here's my card. I'll check back with you again day after tomorrow, but if you turn anything up in the meantime, please call me. It'll be good publicity for you too."

Almost as an afterthought, Ms. Patterson asked everyone there if they had any theories about what the UFO might be, but no one was willing to speculate. "Well, I guess that's it then." She smiled and gathered her things, reminding them again to call her if they learned anything more about the UFO. Then she headed back down the road to the office, waving good-bye.

The three detectives were thrilled to have been interviewed for the newspaper. They had made the front page of the paper after solving their first mystery and hoped they might do so again. Mr. Burnidge, however, was more interested in going fishing. He directed the three detectives to gather fishing poles, bait, a basket for the fish, and lawn chairs. Karen added sunscreen, her favorite wide-brimmed hat, and cans of pop in a cooler to the list. Then they headed off down the path that led to the swimming pool. The manager had said that the best fishing spots in the river were down that path, half a mile beyond the pool.

Karen lingered behind the others, daydreaming of UFOs and aliens. Gradually, though, her thoughts were disturbed by the thrumm, thrumm, thrumm that had disturbed her sleep during the night. It grew louder as they approached the swimming pool. They rounded a bend in the path, and she saw two men in their late teens stretched out in lounge chairs in front of a dome tent. Both men were dressed in ragged blue jeans and dirty T-shirts. And both were completely bald. Their eyes were closed as if they were sleeping. A radio sat on the ground between their lounges, the volume set on high.

Karen hurried her steps to catch up with Kyle and Patrick. "Do you think they're really asleep?" she shouted over the music.

"Probably. They're probably both deaf by now," Patrick answered, also shouting.

"I wonder why no one has complained to the manager."

"Do you really think that would make a difference?"

Karen laughed and they quickened their pace to get past the campsite. The music was eventually drowned out by laughter and splashing from the pool. Then even that noise faded as they entered the woods beyond. Karen breathed a sigh of relief. Loud music was fine at a party, but somehow it seemed out of place in the woods. Determined to enjoy some quiet, Karen hurried ahead of the others — but silence still eluded her. She didn't mind the chattering of the squirrels or the calls of the birds, but the whine of mosquitoes was worse than any human noise. She swiped at one, wishing it would just bite her and leave. Even itching was better than that awful whine.

Suddenly Karen froze. "Kyle," she called softly. He hurried up behind her and put his finger to his lips. He had heard it too. Somewhere up ahead something was making a high-pitched whine, and it wasn't a mosquito. It started, stopped, and then started again.

Patrick, who had been talking to Jonathan and Melanie, now caught up and started to ask what was holding them up. Then he heard it too. "What's that?" he asked in a whisper. Mr. Burnidge, Jonathan, and Melanie stopped, too, and everyone listened intently. The whine lasted only a few seconds each time it occurred. Then suddenly it stopped entirely.

The group waited, listening and listening, but the sound didn't come back. "Let's keep going. Maybe we'll come across whatever was making that sound," suggested Kyle. Mr. Burnidge agreed and they continued down the path.

"That didn't really sound like the UFO," Karen said to Kyle, as they walked along.

"Well, it did and it didn't," Kyle replied. "Both of them sounded like motors, but this was a different pitch."

"Maybe this was from a small scout ship attached to the UFO," Jonathan suggested, with a trace of a smile.

Karen laughed, but felt obliged to protest. "You wait until you've seen it," she said. "It'll convince you."

As the group cleared the trees, they saw another fisherman had beaten them to this spot. Kyle's mouth dropped open as the man pressed a button on the reel of his fishing pole. There was a high-pitched whine as the fishing line shot out into the water without the man so much as bending his wrist.

"I've never seen a fishing pole like that before!" Kyle exclaimed.

The fisherman, tall and thin and in his late twenties, glanced over his shoulder at them. "I should hope not," he said. "This is my own invention."

"How does it work?" Kyle asked, enthralled.

"I'm afraid I'm not at liberty to divulge that," the man replied, but he didn't sound angry that Kyle had asked.

Mr. Burnidge stepped forward. "We're sorry to interrupt your fishing. My name's Thomas Burnidge. This is my son Patrick, his friends, Karen and Kyle Lockhart, my nephew Jonathan, and Melanie Anderson."

The man extended his hand. "I'm Mike Chandler. Nice to meet all of you."

There was an awkward pause. "So, how's the

fishing?" Mr. Burnidge asked, uncomfortable with the silence.

"Well, I'm not catching much," Mr. Chandler replied. "But a friend of mine had some good luck the other day down the river there a bit, if you're looking for a good spot."

His tone indicated he didn't care to continue the conversation, so Mr. Burnidge murmured his thanks. The group turned and headed down the river in the direction Mr. Chandler had suggested.

Kyle couldn't help but wonder about the fishing pole. He stopped and glanced back over his shoulder at Mr. Chandler as the others moved on. Mr. Chandler was casting again. The line shot out in a perfect arc, into the water. Mr. Chandler left it there only a second before reeling it in and casting again. He repeated his actions several times as Kyle watched.

"Great pole," Kyle muttered, "but he's never going to catch any fish if he doesn't ever leave his lure in the water." He turned and trudged along the bank after the others.

Mr. Burnidge had picked out a nice spot just around a bend. The river was about twenty-five feet across at this point and the current swirled the water past gently, yet persistently. Large maple and oak trees provided abundant shade, and there were several big, flat rocks at the river's edge. Karen,

Kyle, and Patrick chose to set up on the rocks, while Mr. Burnidge, Jonathan, and Melanie opted for lawn chairs close by.

For a few minutes everyone was busy, baiting hooks and settling comfortably into their fishing spots. In a short time everyone had their line in the water. Karen looked around and gave a contented sigh. The only sounds were the rush of the water in the river and the occasional call of a bird. It felt so peaceful just to relax and let her mind wander. She began to wonder again what the UFO might be. She didn't really think it was an alien spaceship, so that meant it must be being flown by somebody either at the campground or somebody who lived close by. But why would anybody go to so much trouble just to stir up a little excitement?

As Karen daydreamed, suddenly there was a tug on her line. All thoughts of UFOs instantly disappeared. "I've got something!" she exclaimed. Sure enough her floater was bobbing up and down in the water.

"Reel it in a little," urged Mr. Burnidge.

Karen reeled the line in, trying to keep the tension consistent so that the fish couldn't wriggle free. Slowly she cranked it until the fish broke out of the water. It was round and flat looking — about four or five inches long. Its skin was greenish with small blue gills. Karen moved more quickly, reeling it up. The fish hung at the end of her pole, dancing wildly in the air.

"It's a blue gill," Mr. Burnidge said. He helped Karen take the fish off the hook and put it in the basket, then secured the basket to a dead tree branch dangling in the river and lowered the basket into the water. "They're really tasty. Guess there will be something for dinner tonight."

Soon Patrick and Jonathan followed with fish of their own, and Karen caught a second fish. When Patrick caught his second fish and Kyle hadn't even had a nibble, he got disgusted.

"I must be in a bad spot," he said. "I'm going to move further down." He gathered his things and chose a spot about fifteen feet further down the bank. He studied the water for a moment, then cast his line as far out as he could. As he began gently pulling it back, suddenly it stopped and the floater went down and didn't come up again.

"Hey, look at this!" he called to the others. "I've caught a whopper! Look at how big and heavy it is!" He began reeling it in. It fought him, but Kyle still made steady progress. Slowly he reeled it in. The others all watched eagerly, anxious to see just how big the fish was. Then with a WHOOSH, it came up out of the water. But the thing attached to Kyle's fishing line was not a fish.

Chapter 5

"What is that?" Mr. Burnidge exclaimed.

Everyone stared at the long, metal object which dangled from Kyle's hook. The object was about two feet long, but narrow, perhaps two or three inches wide.

"It looks like a piece of trim off a car," Melanie said.

Kyle reeled the line in and Patrick pulled the object off the end. "Ow!" Patrick yelled. "I stuck my thumb on the end of it. It's sharp."

Jonathan came over and looked at it more closely. "It's jagged here on the end," he said, "as if it broke off from something."

All of them gathered around trying to figure out what the object was and where it could have come from. It was a dull grey, bent and dented some, and the one end did look as if it had broken off from something. There was also a tab about halfway down its length with a small, cut hole that might have been intended for a screw.

"It's just a piece of junk," Mr. Burnidge began when they heard a new voice.

"What'd you catch?" It was Mr. Chandler. He came round the bend, still holding his rod, and sauntered over to the group. "I heard all the commotion and thought I ought to check it out." He reached over and removed the metal object from Patrick's hands. "Now this is a real trophy," he said with a laugh. "I've never caught anything quite as big as this. What do you suppose it is?"

"Probably just some trim off something that somebody threw in the stream," Mr. Burnidge answered.

"It might have come off one of the canoes. You know the manager rents canoes and it wouldn't surprise me that he'd rent canoes that were falling apart. I'm heading back that way now. Would you like for me to drop it by the office?"

Kyle started to protest, but Mr. Burnidge didn't listen. "Go right ahead. I doubt that man will care, but it ought not to be left laying around here."

"That's for sure. Someone could get hurt if they stepped on it." Keeping a tight grasp on the object, Mr. Chandler sauntered off, back around the bend, whistling.

"I bet that was part of the UFO," said Kyle, a little resentful of Mr. Burnidge's disposition of the object.

Mr. Burnidge gave out a big belly laugh. "You kids don't give up, do you?" He laughed again and mopped his forehead with his handkerchief. "Let's see what else we can catch — maybe there's alien fish in here." He picked up his pole and headed back to his chair, still chuckling.

Kyle settled back into his spot and cast his line out into the water, but his mind was no longer on fishing. He stared back at the spot where Mr. Chandler had disappeared from sight and tried to think of an excuse to follow him. He glanced over at Karen and got an idea. With her usual foresight, Karen had brought along a hat to protect her head from the sun, but Kyle had not.

"Mr. Burnidge," he called. "I can really feel the sun on my head. I'm going to run back to the campsite and get a hat."

Mr. Burnidge nodded assent, and Kyle carefully reeled his line in and placed the pole on the bank. Then he hurried down the path, hoping to catch up with Mr. Chandler.

Kyle moved quietly, but quickly through the woods. The only sounds he could hear were bird calls and buzzing insects. Then suddenly he heard voices up ahead on the path. It sounded like someone having an argument.

Kyle couldn't distinguish what was being said, so he moved closer, placing his feet carefully to avoid snapping a twig or stumbling on a rock. Soon he recognized two voices — Mr. Chandler and Ms. Patterson, who is the reporter from the newspaper.

Ms. Patterson was yelling at Mr. Chandler. Kyle edged forward until he could see them.

"How could you be so stupid?" Ms. Patterson was shouting. "You're jeopardizing our whole plan!"

"They don't suspect anything," Mr. Chandler replied, his voice icily angry. "Don't worry about it. And keep your voice down. Do you want the whole campground to hear?"

Ms. Patterson lowered her voice, but it still trembled with hostility. "Mike, this is too important for you to mess it up being careless. This is our big chance." Then to Kyle's surprise, she stepped toward Mr. Chandler, put her arms around his neck and kissed him — a long, lingering kiss.

Embarrassed, Kyle backed away and hid behind a tree.

There was silence for what felt like an eternity, then Kyle heard Mr. Chandler again.

"Don't worry, honey. It's going to be fine. You go back now. We don't want to be seen together." Kyle heard Ms. Patterson head off down the path. He waited and soon Mr. Chandler left as well. Kyle lingered just a minute and then followed.

Kyle easily kept just far enough behind Mr. Chandler so that he wouldn't be noticed. It didn't seem to have even occurred to Mr. Chandler that someone might be following him. He strolled along, whistling off key. Kyle could see that he still held the metal strip in one hand, with his fishing gear in the other.

Mr. Chandler headed straight for the campground office after he passed the swimming pool. He went inside and Kyle ducked behind another tree to wait until he came out. Two minutes later, he did. But he still had the metal strip in his hand. Kyle peeked around the tree trunk, watching to see which way he would go next. Then suddenly a heavy hand clamped itself down on his shoulder and whirled him around.

"Hey! What's the big idea?" Kyle sputtered. Kevin, the manager's son, stood there, confronting him.

"What are you doing here — spying on us?" Kevin leaned forward until his nose practically touched Kyle's. His voice was a low, menacing growl.

Kyle shook himself free from Kevin's grip. From the corner of his eye, he saw Mr. Chandler head off into the woods, toward the campsites, seemingly unaware of Kyle or Kevin. His quarry lost, he confronted Kevin. "I'm not doing anything. Leave me alone."

"You big city hot shots are all alike. Come in here and treat us like dirt and think it don't matter. Well, stay away from me unless you want a fat lip. And if I catch you spying on us again, I'll get my dad to throw you guys out of here. Understand?"

Kyle lost his temper. "I don't think your dad can afford to kick out paying customers. If fact, I don't think he'd like it if I told him you threatened me." Kyle was so angry he didn't stop to think that Kevin was six inches taller and fifty pound heavier than he was — and that it was Patrick who held a brown belt in karate.

Kevin just laughed, unimpressed. "You don't know nothing. Just stay out of my way." He reached out and pushed Kyle hard in the chest. Kyle fell backward, landing in the dirt. Kevin strolled away without looking back.

Kyle struggled to his feet and brushed himself off. He wasn't hurt, but he was angry. He watched Kevin go into the locker room by the swimming pool and then turned and headed for his campsite. He grabbed a baseball cap from his tent, stuck it on his head, and, scowling, traipsed back to join the others, fishing.

The rest of the afternoon was uneventful. Kyle did finally catch a fish and that helped distract his mind from Kevin and Mr. Chandler. Mr. Burnidge was pleased with the fish they had caught and promised to show Patrick, Kyle, and Karen how to fillet them, so they could have fried fish for dinner that night.

On the way back to the campsite, Kyle told

Patrick and Karen about the quarrel he'd overheard between Mr. Chandler and Ms. Patterson. They speculated what it might be about.

"I'll bet it's like Romeo and Juliet," said Karen. "They're passionately in love and their parents don't approve, so they have to meet in secret."

Patrick and Kyle stared at her in disbelief. "Don't you think they're a little old to be worrying about what their parents might think?" Patrick said.

"Well, maybe," Karen replied, but she didn't look convinced.

"I think it's got something to do with the UFO," Kyle said. "Mr. Chandler was pretty quick to grab that metal thing I caught."

"He didn't give it to the manager," Patrick pointed out. "Why wouldn't he do that unless he knew it was part of the UFO?"

"Maybe the manager wasn't there in the office," suggested Karen.

"I don't know," Kyle said, shaking his head, "but I think we ought to keep our eye on him."

They all agreed to that, then turned their attention back to the trail.

Dinner was great that night. The fish fried up perfectly and Jonathan had had the foresight to bury potatoes under the campfire so they had baked potatoes. Karen boiled water and cooked corn-on-the-cob, and Patrick revealed a pan of brownies he'd been saving. After cleaning up, they sang a few songs until it was time to go to the clearing. Mr. Burnidge wanted to see the UFO too, so all six of them hiked into the woods.

The path to the clearing seemed familiar by now to the three detectives, so they raced ahead, checking every now and then to make sure they hadn't lost Jonathan, Melanie, or Mr. Burnidge. Patrick called, "Last one there is a mutant alien!" and it became a race. Squirrels scolded and birds flew up squawking at the noise as the three darted past, but the three friends just laughed and ran on, finally reaching the clearing where they collapsed, laughing and panting. Mr. Burnidge, Jonathan, and Melanie caught up a few minutes later.

Mr. Burnidge had brought a lawn chair, but everyone else sprawled on Karen's quilt and stared up at the sky. There were more clouds than on the previous night, but a few stars could be seen sparkling as the sky darkened into full night.

"We're here earlier than we were last night," Patrick said to his dad. "So we may have to wait awhile."

"That's fine," Mr. Burnidge replied. "It's a beautiful night." He took a deep breath of air. Everyone stared up at the sky.

"I can see the Big Dipper," Kyle said. "But it's not as clear as it was last night." Clouds scuttled across the sky propelled by the wind, blocking their view of the constellation.

There was a moment of silence, which seemed to make Mr. Burnidge uncomfortable. "What would you kids like to do tomorrow?" he asked.

"We want to hike over there," Kyle said pointing east of the clearing. "That's the direction that woman said she saw the UFO go."

"I want to do that too," Karen said. "And I want to go fishing again. But we don't need to do that tomorrow."

"That Chandler guy we met said the manager rents canoes," Jonathan interjected. "I used to do some canoeing a few years ago. Would you like to try that?"

"That sounds great!" Karen said enthusiastically, and the others agreed.

As they talked, the wind changed, becoming suddenly cooler and stronger.

Mr. Burnidge frowned. "Did anyone hear the weather forecast?" he asked.

No one had, but as the wind picked up, the smell of rain became unmistakable.

"Nuts!" said Karen. "I wonder if UFOs fly in the rain."

"They might," said Mr. Burnidge, "but I don't think we should."

"Couldn't we wait a little while," Patrick pleaded.

"It might not rain. And we just got here."

Mr. Burnidge started to say, "All right," but before he could finish the words, drops began to fall from the sky. It was just a light sprinkling, but the steady pace seemed to indicate it wasn't going to quit soon.

"I'm sorry," Mr. Burnidge said. "But I think we'll have to look for the UFO some other night. We'd better head back to the campsite."

Everyone got slowly to their feet and Karen folded up her slightly damp quilt. Mr. Burnidge led the way back down the path. Jonathan and Melanie followed. The three detectives sent one last look at the sky and fell in behind them.

By the time they got back to the campsite, the rain was falling harder. Karen and Melanie ducked into their tent to change into dry clothes, while the others changed in the big tent. No one felt like sleeping yet, so Karen and Melanie joined the others in the big tent.

Jonathan strummed a few notes on his guitar and Patrick started to sing with him. Everyone joined in and their spirits lifted.

"It hasn't been showing up every night anyway, so it probably wouldn't have come tonight," Kyle said, as the song came to a conclusion. "We'll go back tomorrow night."

"Wait until you see it," said Patrick to his dad. "It

really is spooky." The three detectives sat still a minute, remembering what they had seen.

"I'd like a soda," Karen said. "Anybody else want one?"

Everybody did, so Karen grabbed an umbrella and a flashlight and hurried out to the van. The cooler with soda and perishable food was in the back of the van.

Karen pulled open the door to the van and stared in. Then she yelled, "Mr. Burnidge! Come quick!"

Mr. Burnidge barrelled out of the tent, closely followed by Jonathan, Melanie, and the two boys,

heedless of the rain. Karen pointed into the van. "Look!" she said, and her voice trembled.

The back of the van was empty. Everything they had stored in it was gone.

Chapter 6

Predictably the manager, whose name they learned was Edwin Turner, offered neither help nor sympathy. In fact, he acted as if Mr. Burnidge had gotten robbed just to force him to come out into the rain. He finally agreed to call the sheriff's department, but he didn't offer any hope that the sheriff would actually be able to do anything.

"Ya leave your stuff jest laying anywhere and ya don't expect no one ta take it? City slickers. Always think youse so smart, but I seen brighter mules."

The deputy sheriff who arrived thirty minutes later was more polite, but he confirmed that it was unlikely that they'd be able to locate the perpetrator. He looked at the van and checked around the campsite, then wrote everything in his notebook. He didn't find anything, but he was, however, able to give them some information Mr. Turner had neglected to mention.

"There have been a rash of petty thefts out here in the last several weeks. But we haven't been able to come up with any clues as to who's involved. It isn't even necessarily the same thief each time. Most everyone leaves stuff just laying around in a campground, and somebody walking past might not be able to resist the temptation. Mr. Turner says twenty-seven of the forty campsites are filled tonight. Any one of the campers could have come past here and just helped themselves. And it doesn't even have to be someone staying here. It could be a staff person or a visitor."

"Or an alien," said Mr. Burnidge with a weary smile.

The deputy laughed. "Yeah, I heard about that UFO out here. We came out and looked around after it was first sighted. I never did see the thing, but I guess a lot of people have."

"We saw it last night," Karen said. "It was great."

The deputy smiled and closed his notebook.

"Well, I'm sorry I can't offer much help. There just isn't anything to go on. Next time be sure to lock your van."

Mr. Burnidge scowled, but he acknowledged that the deputy was right. After the man left, they decided it was time for bed.

*   *   *   *   *   *   *   *   *   *   *

It rained most of the night, but finally stopped in the early hours of the morning. Karen was grateful that apparently the rain had discouraged the two young men from playing their radio all night. The air was hot and muggy as everyone gathered for breakfast. Mr. Burnidge announced that he planned to visit the camp store to replace the supplies they'd lost. Fortunately there hadn't been much else besides food in the back of the van. Mr. Burnidge wasn't happy about buying things from the camp store — he remembered what the place looked like — but there was little choice unless he drove all the way back to Preston. Melanie and Jonathan decided to accompany him.

Karen, Kyle, and Patrick decided that seeing the outside of the camp store was the closest they wanted to come to it. Mr. Burnidge agreed they could go hiking, so they headed off into the woods to look for the UFO.

They followed the familiar path to the clearing. It was muddy from the rain, but not enough to slow them down. After reaching the clearing, they changed directions, pushing their way through the wet underbrush in an easterly direction. Kyle took the lead, with Karen close behind him and Patrick bringing up the rear. Kyle studied the plants carefully as he tried to follow what appeared to be an old trail. He didn't want to spend the rest of the week itching from poison ivy.

Luck favored them. About ten minutes after leaving the clearing, the faint trail intersected with a dirt path. Without hesitation, Kyle turned onto the path, ignoring the soft squishing sounds his shoes made as he tramped through the mud.

"How do you know this is the right direction to go?" Karen asked, wrinkling her nose in distaste as her shoe stuck in the mud.

"As long as it's leading away from the main campground, it's worth investigating," Kyle replied.

The path sloped downward, winding around until they reached the river at a point upstream from where they had gone fishing. The rain had raised the river level, and the water rushed over the rocks, splashing and tumbling. Limestone bluffs topped with trees bordered the river at this point, but the path continued along the river bank. This part of the trail had caught the early morning sunshine and, to Karen's relief, there were only occasional patches of mud. The three detectives followed along, studying the rocky cliffs to their right and the turbulent water to their left.

"Hey look," Karen called after they had been hiking along the river's edge for twenty minutes. "There's another path over there." She pointed to a faint trail which curved off the main path, up the side of the bluff. "Do you suppose there's anything up there?"

"Well, there's certainly nothing down here," Patrick replied. "Let's see where it goes."

The new trail was more difficult to follow. Mud wasn't the problem. There were so many rocks on the path, there wasn't room for anyone. But the incline was rather steep and the path not as well worn. The track wound up the face of the bluff in an "s" pattern, moving across the side, then curving back around on a slightly higher path and going back across. Karen stumbled over a tree root and would have fallen if Patrick hadn't caught her arm. Kyle did slip on some loose rock, but he didn't slide far. All three were panting by the time they had gotten halfway to the top of the bluff.

"Whew!" Karen exclaimed. "It's too hot to work this hard."

"You know," Kyle said, studying the way the path curved, "I don't think it would be much harder to go straight up and it certainly would be faster."

"I'm not sure we should get off the path," Patrick said hesitantly.

"We wouldn't be off for long. See how the path goes? It keeps switching back on itself. If we went straight up we'd run into part of the path every few feet."

Patrick and Karen could see the logic of this. And they were both so hot and tired they would have agreed to try almost anything to get to the top faster. They chose a spot in the middle of the path. The path led off to the left, but they turned off it and climbed straight up, leaving the path behind. It was even tougher going now. Karen used both hands to climb over a big rock and Patrick got tangled in some weeds, but in a few minutes they found another bend of the path just above them.

"See," said Kyle. "That was a lot faster. Let's do it again."

Instead of following the new path as it led off to the right, they plunged once again straight up the side of the bluff. The terrain was even rougher here, though, and they couldn't always go straight up. A large rock in their path forced them to angle to the right, and then a dense patch of bushes forced them further right.

"Shouldn't we have run into the path by now?" Karen asked after a few minutes.

"I don't know," Kyle replied, his voice sounding troubled.

Patrick swatted a mosquito. "It's bound to be up ahead. Let's keep going."

They kept on, forcing their way through the underbrush, but the path didn't appear. Finally, they had to stop to catch their breath.

"Maybe we should try to go back," Karen suggested. She was hot and tired and just a little scared.

"Well, we're practically at the top now," Kyle answered. "Even if there isn't a path, we can't get lost if we keep going up. We've got to get to the top eventually."

Patrick lent his support to Kyle, so Karen reluctantly agreed. Ten minutes later Kyle admitted they were lost.

Somehow hearing Kyle admit they were lost made Karen feel better. Now they could solve the problem. "Let's try calling for help," Karen suggested. "Maybe somebody else is up here and will hear us."

"It wouldn't hurt," said Patrick. Kyle just nodded his head.

"Is anybody out there?" Karen yelled. She paused, but there was no reply.

"Help!!" shouted Kyle and Patrick at the same time. Nothing.

Kyle paused a moment, listening. "Hey, I can still hear the river," he said. "If we go downhill, heading for the sound, we're sure to find the path."

"That's what you said about going up," Karen muttered, but she agreed it made sense.

The three began working their way back in the direction they had come from. Going downhill, retracing their steps was a little easier than forcing their way up had been. Then suddenly Patrick slipped.

Karen screamed as Patrick plunged down the hill. He grabbed at a bush trying to stop himself, but it pulled free, roots and all. Rocks and mud and leaves flew about as Patrick slid faster and then disappeared from sight.

Karen and Kyle hurried as quickly as they dared, trying to catch up with Patrick. They could still hear him scattering rocks and such as he tumbled down, then suddenly it was quiet.

"Patrick! Are you all right?" the twins called frantically. They pushed through some bushes and saw Patrick, sitting in the dirt brushing himself off.

"I found the path," he said ruefully.

Patrick had landed in the middle of a broad, well-traveled path. His fall had given him a few scratches and bruises, and he was covered with mud and twigs and leaves, but he wasn't hurt. He stood up and brushed himself off as best he could.

Karen and Kyle closed their eyes in a prayer of thanks that he was all right and then studied the new trail. It gave them a choice — back down to the river or up the bluff. Kyle looked at the others and grinned. "You guys want to try it again?" he asked.

"Why not?" they replied. Karen added, "But no more shortcuts!"

Once more they climbed. Soon Kyle pulled ahead of the other two, anxious to see where the trail was leading. But instead of going to the top of the bluff, it curved around the side of the bluff and began to slope downhill.

"Doesn't anybody believe in nice level paths?" Karen grumbled as she hurried along, trying to keep up with Kyle. "Slow down!" she yelled as Kyle rounded a bend and disappeared from sight. She scratched at a mosquito bite and quickened her pace. So did Patrick.

But when Karen and Patrick finally rounded the bend and caught up with Kyle, they stopped short in surprise. Kyle stood there too, and all three stared at the small cabin they'd found.

Someone had once lived here they determined as they moved closer and examined the cabin. The structure had been built with huge logs, now weathered with age. There was only one window, but there were two doors, one in front and one in back. The front door stood open, so the three detectives went inside. There was just one room. A cot without bedding sat in one corner and there was a small table with two benches. A few dishes sat on shelves on the far wall and a big cast iron pot hung on a spit in a large fireplace. Dirt, dust, and cobwebs were everywhere, but tracks of mud indicated that someone else had been there recently. Kyle examined the fireplace and announced that someone had built a fire there within the last few days.

"Maybe this is a backpacker station," Karen suggested.

"I don't think so," Kyle replied thoughtfully. "There'd be some kind of sign if it were, and it would probably be used more frequently. This place looks like nobody's been here for years, except for whoever made the fire and tracked in the mud."

"Probably somebody took cover here last night in the rain," Patrick said, continuing to study the cabin interior.

The mud hadn't left any recognizable footprint, but the boys examined the floor anyway, looking for clues. Karen drifted out the back door. When she saw the grassy area behind the cabin, she let out a yell. "Kyle! Patrick! Come quick!"

The two boys hurried out after her, then all three stared in amazement. The grass was thick and green in the back yard — except in one spot. Right in the middle of the grass there was a large, circular indentation, as if a large, circular object had rested there.

"Wow!" said Patrick in a hushed voice.

"That has to be from the UFO," Kyle said, also speaking in a whisper.

Slowly the three detectives walked over to the impression. The circle was about eight feet in diameter. The grass was crushed evenly in the area, seemingly indicating that the craft did not have legs or any protrusions on its bottom.

"Now what?" Karen asked.

Kyle knelt down next to the circle and sniffed. "I don't smell anything unusual, but that doesn't mean anything. The rain last night probably would have washed away any smells."

Patrick walked slowly around the circle. Karen and Kyle followed. They studied the circle from every angle.

"You know," Kyle said. "I remember reading about UFO circles in those books I got from the library. Farmers sometimes find circles in the middle of their fields. Just all of a sudden one morning there's this big circle with no path leading into it or out of it. One guy in Iowa found a ninety foot circle in the middle of his soybeans. They never did figure out what caused it. Though that

circle seemed to have been burned there. This is just crushed grass."

For a minute the three detectives just stood there staring down at the circle. Then Patrick looked at his watch. "It's probably time to head back for lunch," he said reluctantly.

Kyle sighed and agreed. "Anyway, wait until we tell your dad and Jonathan and Melanie about this."

The hike back was uneventful. The path led right back to the river at a spot only a little further downriver from the first path up the bluff. When they reached the campsite, they saw Jonathan and Melanie just putting some hot dogs on the grill. Mr. Burnidge was setting the picnic table with paper plates and napkins.

"You'll never guess what we found!" Karen exclaimed as soon as they were within earshot. "We found a spot where the UFO landed!"

Mr. Burnidge just laughed and sighed, but Jonathan and Melanie demanded all the details. Patrick, Kyle, and Karen filled them in, glossing over the part where they left the trail and got lost. Jonathan was the most interested in the cabin.

"Think you could find that spot again?" he asked.

"Of course," Kyle answered.

"It would be fun later to have a look at it."

Everyone seemed to have an appetite and lunch was finished in short order. After lunch Karen, Kyle, and Patrick cleaned up the few dishes. Jonathan settled comfortably into a lawn chair and picked up the newspaper he'd gotten at the camp store.

"Hey! Guess what?" Jonathan said as he turned the page.

"The Cubs won yesterday?" Patrick guessed.

"Don't be ridiculous. The Mets beat them six to two. No, look here. There's an article about the UFO."

The article was in the center of the fourth page of the paper and had Darlene Patterson's byline. The article was not very long, but the headline was in

big bold letters: **UFO Sighted Over Campground.** Everyone crowded close while Jonathan read the article aloud.

Vacationers at Sunrise Campground, ten miles northwest of Preston, have added a new attraction to the usual round of swimming, hiking, and canoeing: watching a UFO. Over the last three weeks more than thirty campers have observed strange lights in the sky over the campground.

The circular pattern of red and white lights was first observed in late July. The sheriff's department reports that no official explanation has been accepted to account for the lights.

The short article continued, including a quote from Kevin, the manager's son, who was cited as being firmly convinced the UFO was from outer space. Karen and Kyle, and Patrick were not mentioned.

"She didn't even mention us," Karen said dejectedly as they finished reading.

"Probably her editor cut out the stuff on us." Kyle, too, was disappointed.

"I wonder if we should call her and tell her about the circle," said Patrick.

"Let's wait and see if we can come up with anything else first," Karen said.

By this time everything from lunch was put away;

Mr. Burnidge had a surprise. "While we were at the store, I arranged to rent some canoes for this afternoon. You kids interested in taking them out?"

Karen and Kyle, and Patrick responded enthusiastically, all thoughts of the UFO being temporarily pushed aside.

*   *   *   *   *   *   *   *   *   *   *

Kevin drove the six of them up to the boat launch in a beat-up van, towing the canoes behind on a special trailer.

"I'll be at the pick-up point at 4:00 pm," he promised in a surly tone of voice, after he and Jonathan had unloaded the canoes. "Any idiot could find it. You only go under one bridge the whole trip. After you go under, pull over to the right bank and you'll see the road."

"Did the rain affect the water level?" Mr. Burnidge asked. "Are there any spots where we might have trouble?"

Kevin rolled his eyes. "A baby could navigate this river," he said. Then he hopped back in the van and drove off without a backward look. Mr. Burnidge scowled after him, but then forced a smile on his face as he turned around and saw Patrick and the others watching him.

Everyone put on their life jackets and hats.

Mr. Burnidge had bought small coolers for each canoe, each of which held a six-pack of soda. These were loaded, along with suntan lotion. Then Mr. Burnidge and Patrick got in the first canoe, Melanie and Karen jumped into the second, and Jonathan and Kyle followed in the third. Everything was set, so they pushed off into the river.

The air was cooler out on the river and a light breeze helped too, though it threatened to blow Karen's hat off. The current was a little swifter than anything Karen had been on before, but she and Melanie had no trouble paddling their canoe. "This is great!" she called to Mr. Burnidge.

For a while, Karen and Melanie paddled vigorously, laughing as they passed the other two canoes. They got as far ahead as they could and still remain in sight of the others. Then their arms, which were unaccustomed to this form of exercise, began to protest, so they drifted, just using the paddles to steer as necessary. The river was about thirty feet wide here. Trees lined the bank on the right, limestone cliffs rose high above them on the left. Karen and Melanie glided along enjoying the quiet. The only sounds were the rushing of the water and the calls of the birds. It felt very relaxing. Karen reached down and let her fingers trail in the cool water. "Wouldn't it be great to stay out here forever," she said to Melanie. Melanie agreed.

The peace didn't last forever, though. It didn't even last half an hour. Gradually, Karen became aware that the sound of the water was growing louder.

"Sounds like some rapids ahead," Melanie said.

"All right!" Karen exclaimed. "Let's show those guys how to do white water with style!"

The rapids had been caused by a narrowing of the river. The same amount of water had to get through a smaller space so it moved more swiftly. It was exciting to skim along, the spray blanketing Karen and Melanie with a fine mist, the speed exhilarating. Everything was going fine. Karen and Melanie worked together well, keeping the canoe to the center of the river. Then suddenly, they rounded a bend and there was a big rock sticking up in the middle of the channel.

"Paddle to the right!" Melanie called.

Karen paddled as hard as she could. In fact, she paddled too vigorously. The front of the canoe veered right, avoiding the rock, but the current caught the back of the canoe. The canoe spun around and they ended up facing backward, heading swiftly downstream.

Chapter 7

"I don't think this is the way it's supposed to work," Karen muttered. "In fact, I'm sure this is wrong." She was staring back the way they had come, glad that the bend temporarily blocked them from the view of the other two canoes.

"Don't worry!" Melanie yelled. "Stick your paddle in the water and hold it still, like a rudder."

Karen did and Melanie began paddling as hard as she could, intending to reverse them in the same way that they'd gotten turned around in the first place. They began to swing around, but the activity brought them closer to the river bank where a dead tree branch stuck out over the water. The branch appeared to have been struck by lightning. It was black with just a few dead leaves on it and it hung only half attached. Instinctively, Karen reached up with her paddle and shoved at the branch, attempting to push the canoe away from it. But they were going too fast. The impact caused the canoe to flip, dumping Karen, Melanie, and all their things into the water.

Both Karen and Melanie bobbed up immediately,

thanks to their life jackets and the fact that both were good swimmers, but the sight that met their eyes was discouraging. The canoe was upside down and rapidly disappearing downstream, being swept along by the current. The paddles and seat cushions were following it. Karen was relieved to see that the cooler could float, but it, too, was speeding downstream. So were her and Melanie's hats.

Melanie checked first to be sure that Karen was all right. Karen's heart was beating much faster and stronger than usual, but she wasn't really scared. The whole thing had happened too quickly for that. She assured Melanie that she was fine. In fact the cold water felt good. Then the two of them struck out after their things, swimming as quickly as they could.

The hats had completely disappeared, but they were the least important of the items they'd lost. Karen caught up to the cooler, but then found she couldn't hold onto it and swim at the same time. She tossed it up on the bank, intending to come back for it. Melanie called that they should try to get the canoe first, so she swam toward it.

By this time the other two canoes had rounded the bend and the men saw what had happened. Kyle called out, "Are you guys hurt?" Concern made his voice quiver just a little.

Karen shouted back, "We're fine. Can you help get our stuff?"

Kyle gave Karen a thumbs up, and he and Jonathan steered toward the seat cushions while Patrick and Mr. Burnidge chased the paddles, swerving over to the bank to grab the cooler on their way past.

Karen and Melanie reached their canoe and guided it toward a low spot on the bank. The current fought them, but they were past the swiftest part of the river and they managed to drag it over. They scrambled up the bank and together they flipped the canoe right side up, dumping out most of the water.

"You willing to get back in?" Melanie asked Karen, only half joking.

"I may be soggy, but my spirit is unquenched," Karen replied with a grin. She slid back in the canoe just as Patrick and Mr. Burnidge paddled up.

"I think you'll find these useful," teased Patrick as he handed them back their paddles.

Karen shook her head, spraying Patrick with droplets of water from her hair. "Why, thank you," she said, and then she stuck her tongue out at him.

"Are you two sure that you're all right?" Mr. Burnidge asked.

"Yes, we're fine," Melanie answered. "It was just a freak accident." Kyle and Jonathan paddled over, and they all insisted on hearing exactly what had happened. Karen was embarrassed and let Melanie do the talking. Kyle didn't tease her though, and Mr. Burnidge seemed concerned about finishing the trip.

"We're fine, really," Karen said. "I was wishing I could do a little swimming. I just didn't expect to do it with all my clothes on."

Mr. Burnidge allowed himself to be convinced. Jonathan offered to trade places with Melanie, but neither Karen nor Melanie would agree. In fact, Melanie muttered something under her breath that sounded suspiciously like, "Male chauvinist."

The journey continued without further mishap. Karen and Melanie stayed closer to the other two canoes this time, but there were no more rapids. The hot sun soon dried their clothes, and though Melanie wished aloud that she had a comb for her hair, it seemed their unexpected dip had not caused any real problems. They stopped once on a sand bar where they built a sand castle, but other than that they paddled along quickly, enjoying the scenery and the fresh air. When they crossed under the bridge Kevin had mentioned and saw the pick-up point, everyone was disappointed.

"Next time let's make it a longer trip," Patrick suggested.

"Our trip was even faster than Kevin expected,"

Mr. Burnidge said, glancing down at his watch. "He said he'd be here at 4:00, but it's only 3:30. I guess we'll just have to wait."

They pulled the canoes up out of the water and stacked their supplies neatly to one side. They were surprised to see another canoe with two life jackets resting to the side.

"Kevin didn't mention that anyone else was canoeing. I wonder if they're also from the campground," Mr. Burnidge said.

It took only a few minutes to take care of their own things. The three detectives didn't feel like just sitting and waiting for Kevin to show up. They wandered up a dirt incline and found the road just over a rise. There were some woods across the road and a parked car, but Patrick said his dad wouldn't want them to go too far away, so they came back. Off to either side of the pick-up point, there were a few trees and large rocks.

"Mind if we explore over there a bit?" Karen asked Mr. Burnidge, gesturing off to the right.

"All right, but don't go far," he said.

Kyle and Patrick followed Karen into the trees. Karen scrambled up on top of a large rock close to the river's edge. "Hey," she called, "Pretty good view up here."

Kyle and Patrick climbed up next to her and looked around. Kyle noticed a spot of blue on the far bank of the river. "Look, Karen," he said pointing to it, "There's your hat."

Karen grinned. "Great! Let's go get it."

They jumped down from the rock and hurried back to the canoes. Mr. Burnidge gave them permission to go across the bridge, though he added an unnecessary caution to be careful crossing over.

The far bank was similar to the one they'd been on. Karen easily located her hat. "All it needs is to dry out and it'll be good as new," she said, picking it up.

Kyle noticed a path heading into the woods and wandered toward it, wondering where it went. He took a few steps and then noticed what appeared to be a pile of clothes lying on the trail further ahead. He stared at the pile for a moment and then suddenly, he raced down the path, calling to Patrick and Karen to follow. Piles of clothes didn't groan and move!

Darlene Patterson, the reporter from the newspaper, lay on the path, apparently just recovering consciousness. Kyle was the first to reach her, but Karen and Patrick were close behind.

"What should we do?" Karen asked Kyle.

"Patrick, run get your dad and everybody. We'll stay with her."

Karen knelt down next to the young woman and

took her hand. The pulse, she was relieved to notice, was strong and steady and there wasn't any blood or any other sign of injury. She wondered what had happened.

Ms. Patterson was dressed as she had been the day before, wearing a linen skirt and matching jacket. The young woman groaned again and her eyes flickered open. "My head," she moaned.

"It's OK," Karen said softly. "We're going to help you."

Patrick and the others arrived, and Mr. Burnidge took charge.

"You can try to sit up," he said, "but go slowly. What happened?"

Ms. Patterson pulled herself up and rubbed the back of her head. "I don't know what happened. I was just hiking around, looking for clues about the UFO, and," she paused and looked around with a puzzled expression on her face, "and I guess I must have fallen. But I don't know how I could have hit the back of my head." She reached her hand up and gently probed a bump on the back of her head. "I'm feeling better now." As if to prove that, she struggled to her feet.

"Don't push yourself too quickly," Mr. Burnidge said. "You'll need to see a doctor."

"I'm fine. Really." She began looking about on the ground as if searching for something.

"Did you lose something?" Mr. Burnidge asked. "Were you carrying a purse?"

"No, I had . . . no, there wasn't anything."

"Is that your canoe over at the pick-up point?" Jonathan asked.

"No. I drove. My car is parked across the bridge."

"Well, I don't think you should try to drive home," Mr. Burnidge said. "Why don't you let one of us drive you."

Ms. Patterson agreed to let Jonathan drive her back home. They crossed back over the bridge,

Ms. Patterson leaning on Mr. Burnidge's arm. Just as they reached the road, two young men sauntered out of the far woods. Karen recognized them as the ones who had been playing the loud music back at the campground. She was certain because of their bald heads.

"Hey! What's happening?" one of them called.

"This young lady has been hurt," Mr. Burnidge replied, somewhat frostily. It appeared he, too, recognized them.

"Bummer," said the second young man.

Mr. Burnidge scowled and started to say something, but just then everyone was distracted by the arrival of Kevin and the van.

"Kevin, my man, you're late," the first young man called to him.

"Big deal. Five minutes," Kevin replied.

"Well, I hope she was a fox," said the second young man, and the two of them laughed uproariously.

"Where'd she come from?" Kevin asked, looking at Ms. Patterson.

"She was hiking and fell and injured herself," Mr. Burnidge replied. "My nephew is going to drive her home."

"Oh. Good. I'm not supposed to take anybody in the van except people staying at the campground."

Mr. Burnidge shook his head at Kevin's only concern and helped Ms. Patterson get to her car, which was the one the three detectives had noticed earlier. Jonathan and the two young men loaded the canoes onto the boat trailer. Then Jonathan drove off with Ms. Patterson and the others climbed into the van.

"Do you think she was telling the truth?" Karen asked Kyle and Patrick, as Kevin started the van and pulled onto the road. She spoke in a low voice. The two bald young men were joking around with Kevin and appeared completely uninterested in anyone else, but Karen didn't want them to overhear anything.

"What do you mean?" Kyle asked.

"That she was looking around for clues about the UFO. Her story already ran. The paper wouldn't do two stories on it, and wouldn't she have another assignment to do?"

"You've got a point," Patrick said thoughtfully. "I wonder what she was really doing. Must have something to do with whatever she was fighting with that Mr. Chandler about."

"And do you think she really fell and hit her head — or do you think somebody hit her?"

"I bet it was them." Kyle jerked his head toward the two young men who were laughing raucously at something Kevin had said.

The three detectives continued to discuss the case until they got back to the campground, but they weren't able to produce any reasonable theories. Karen was surprised that the campsite felt so much like home after such a short time. She and Melanie ducked into their tent to change their clothes and comb their hair, while Kyle, Patrick and Mr. Burnidge began fixing dinner.

Even canned beef stew smells good heated over a campfire, Karen thought, stepping out of the tent a few minutes later, pulling a brush through her hair. I could get to like this.

Melanie had finished changing faster and was helping Kyle and Patrick set paper plates and cups on the picnic table.

"Need any help?" Karen started to say, but then she stopped and gazed in horror at the edge of the woods. "D-d-d-don't anybody move!" she stammered.

Naturally, everyone spun around and stared at the spot that held Karen transfixed. Out from the woods trotted a mother skunk, followed by three baby skunks.

As one, everybody ran for Mr. Burnidge's van. They tumbled in and slammed the door.

The skunks were actually quite beautiful, glowing black coats with the traditional white stripe and luminous black eyes. The babies were as cute as baby kittens, each a perfect replica of its mother. They appeared to be completely indifferent to the humans. They waltzed into the campsite, sniffing at the tents, the chairs, and other items scattered about as if it had all been set up just for their approval. The people, trapped in their cage, watched helplessly.

"This has not been one of my better days," Karen muttered, her nose pressed against the window, watching the animals. "Lost. Almost drowned. And now skunks!"

For a full ten minutes the skunks investigated the campsite. Then the sound of an approaching car startled them and they darted back into the woods. Jonathan got out of a taxi and walked over to the van.

"What on earth are all of you doing in there?" he asked.

*   *   *   *   *   *   *   *   *   *   *

Dinner had gotten a little scorched, thanks to the skunks, but it still tasted good. After they cleaned up the dishes, Jonathan and Melanie were eager to hike to the clearing to see if the UFO would return. Karen thought longingly of her nice soft bed at home and fantasized about getting ten or twelve hours of uninterrupted sleep. But Kyle and Patrick were sure the UFO would be back that night, and she knew she couldn't stand to miss it if it did.

They locked everything up in the van and then headed once again down the path to the clearing. They decided not to take their cameras this time, figuring that they could study what the UFO looked like better if they weren't trying to focus a lens. Everyone had flashlights, Mr. Burnidge carried a lawn chair, and Karen clutched her quilt.

The clearing was brilliantly illuminated by the moon and stars. As Karen stared up, she felt peace steal over her and she was glad that she had come, even if the UFO didn't show up. She spread the quilt out and lay on her back gazing up at the sky in awe. Jonathan took Melanie's hand and they sat together on the edge of the quilt, her head resting upon his shoulder. Mr. Burnidge relaxed in his lawn chair. Kyle and Patrick, however, didn't seem to feel the same mood. They wandered restlessly about the clearing, glancing up at the sky every few seconds.

"If the aliens have any sense at all, they'll be out for a spin on a night like this," Jonathan said, after a short while.

"It was worth the hike whether they show up or not," Melanie replied softly.

A light breeze rustled the leaves and then they heard it — a low buzz just like they had heard that first night.

"That's it!" Patrick exclaimed excitedly, and everyone leaped to their feet, searching the sky.

The circle of red and white lights approached from the north. In the light of the moon, Karen could see clearly that the UFO really did look like all the cartoon representations of a flying saucer. It was silver and seemed to be made out of metal. The bottom was round with the red and white lights set on the edge of the rim. A round dome sat on top, and Karen was fairly sure she could see a window in it. It circled overhead once and then twice, as if showing off, and then zoomed away, in the direction it had come from.

There was a moment of silence. Then Mr. Burnidge said, "Well, I wouldn't have believed it. I've never seen anything like that in my life."

Melanie and Jonathan exchanged glances, shaking their heads. "That certainly was impressive," Jonathan said.

"It's got to be a model somebody's flying," Kyle said with certainty. "I got a pretty good look at it this time."

"It definitely wasn't swamp gas," Jonathan said.

Everyone laughed and they all began talking at once, comparing what they had seen. Everyone agreed it looked just like a cartoon UFO.

They waited half an hour to see if the UFO would

return, but it didn't. Finally Mr. Burnidge said they should return to camp. He folded up his lawn chair and Karen gathered her quilt. They walked slowly back to the tents, each person lost in thought. They checked, somewhat nervously, to be sure no one had been in their campsite, and then everyone settled in quickly for sleep.

* * * * * * * * * * *

All three detectives were up early the next morning.

"We only have two days left to solve this thing," Patrick said, as they sat at the picnic table eating cereal. "What do we have so far?"

"The pictures should come back today," Kyle said. "Jonathan said they could be picked up after 3:30."

"That'll be great," Patrick replied, "but even if your pictures are better than I think mine will turn out, it really won't help much. We already know we saw red and white lights in the sky. We need to know where to look in the daytime. Where could the UFO be now?"

Karen and Kyle thought about everything that had happened. There had to be some kind of clue.

"The river," Karen said suddenly. "Every clue we've had points to the river. The UFO flies around

112

near the river. Kyle caught a piece of it in the river. It landed by that cabin up the bluff from the river. And it was right by the river that Ms. Patterson got hit on the head."

"We don't know that she was hit on the head," Kyle protested, but he and Patrick were struck by Karen's logic.

"Let's go back there today," Patrick suggested. "I bet Jonathan wouldn't mind driving us back to the bridge, and then we could look around and find whatever it was that made somebody hit Ms. Patterson on the head."

"She said she fell," Kyle objected, but Karen and Patrick ignored him.

"All right! There has to be something there or somebody wouldn't have tried to scare her away." Karen was enthusiastic.

Kyle opened his mouth and then closed it. He knew when to give up.

Jonathan did agree to drive them back to the bridge. Mr. Burnidge cautioned them to stay together and keep on the paths. The three detectives exchanged guilty looks and promised they would.

The bridge and river bank looked just the same as they had the day before. Jonathan dropped the three detectives off and promised to return for them in two hours, just before lunch.

The three detectives crossed the bridge and headed down the path where they had found Ms. Patterson. It led a short way into the woods and then curved back along the bluffs by the river. Kyle forged ahead, eagerly searching for a clue. Patrick wasn't far behind him.

"Come on, Karen," Kyle called. "We only have two hours and there's a lot of area here to be searched."

"I'll search my way. You search yours," Karen called back. "You're bound to miss stuff going so fast."

Kyle shrugged his shoulders and kept going.

"This is a nice hike even if we don't find anything," Karen said, as she strolled along, enjoying the scenery. "Look at all these weird rocks."

The limestone cliffs had been carved by wind and rain into some unusual configurations. One looked just like a man with a very large nose and another like a bird with its head tilted to one side.

"What are we looking for?" Patrick asked after about ten minutes of searching.

"Anything unusual," Kyle replied. He studied a branch that had been broken off a tree. "Like this could have been damaged by the UFO going through here. We should also keep an eye out for where somebody could hide a flying saucer."

"Like a cave?" Karen called, her tone of voice suddenly amused. She had kept the boys in eyesight, but she still lagged behind them.

"Yeah," Kyle said, "or a shed or a clearing surrounded by big trees." He continued darting his glance here, there and everywhere.

"Well, how about checking out that cave?" Karen said. She pointed to a dark shadow which indicated an opening in the cliff. Both boys had walked right past without seeing it.

"Wow!" said Patrick. Kyle just shook his head.

The three detectives approached the cave slowly. The opening was set at an angle to the path and was larger than it had first appeared. Sunlight streamed in from the entrance revealing a large cavern of limestone. There were no stalactites or stalagmites or other cave formations. But right in the middle of the cave sat the UFO!

Chapter 8

The three detectives moved cautiously into the cave and, as their eyes adjusted to the gloom of the cavern, examined the UFO. Up close the flying saucer was a disappointment. For one thing, it just wasn't that big. It couldn't have been more than eight feet in diameter and stood no more than four feet tall. It did look like a traditional flying saucer, though. It had a round dome sitting on top of a bottom piece, so that the two parts looked like two saucers put together, but its silver surface was

dented and scratched. There were no doors or windows. The red and white lights actually were Christmas tree lights. It certainly hadn't flown here from another planet. In fact, Karen was surprised it was able to fly over the campground.

Kyle was the first to reach out and touch it.

"Well, what do you know," he said in a whisper. "It's real." Karen giggled.

Patrick stepped toward it and stepped on something. He twisted his ankle and almost fell, but caught his balance in time. "Look, Kyle," he said, reaching down and picking up a long metal object up from the cave floor. "It's that metal thing you caught when we were fishing."

Kyle and Karen studied it. Kyle was sure it was the same one. "And it did come off this thing. See, right here." He pointed to a strip of trim above the lights. There was a section missing just the size of the piece Kyle had caught. Patrick held the piece up to the spot and it matched exactly.

Patrick held onto the metal strip and turned his attention back to the UFO. He reached up and rapped on the side of the craft. A hollow echo came back. Then the three detectives heard another sound, a cry like the whimper of an animal caught in a trap.

"What's that?" Patrick whispered.

"There could be an animal in here," said Karen,

quickly looking around.

"It came from back there," Kyle said, pointing to a dark area behind the UFO. He stepped cautiously in that direction, the others right behind him. As he drew closer to the shadow, he could make out the figure of a person lying on the ground, bound and gagged. All three detectives rushed over.

It was Darlene Patterson. She was conscious, but a bandanna had been stuffed in her mouth, her hands were tied behind her back, and her ankles were bound together.

"Get her untied," Kyle snapped.

Karen pulled the bandanna from Ms. Patterson's mouth while the boys worked on untying the ropes.

"Thank goodness!" Ms. Patterson exclaimed, as soon as she could. "Quickly now. He'll be back soon."

"Who?" asked Karen, but the answer didn't come from Ms. Patterson. It came from the cave entrance.

"Me." Kevin Turner stood in the cave opening, looking at the four of them in disgust. "Little Miss Snoopy Nose here just couldn't stop poking around. And neither could you three clowns, so now you can all keep each other company." Kevin spoke confidently, with a smirk on his face because there was a gun in his hand.

He swaggered over to a large pile of items laying near the cave wall, never once taking his eyes off the four of them. He grabbed a couple of ropes from the pile and flung them to Kyle. "Tie up your sister and your friend," he said in a menacing voice. "Unless you'd rather I put a bullet in one of you."

Kyle reluctantly picked up a rope and looped it around Karen's wrists.

"Not that way, idiot," Kevin snapped. "Behind her back. And don't try anything else cute. I'm going to be checking those ropes and the looser they are, the harder I'm going to kick her."

Kyle tied up Karen and Patrick, not daring to use a trick knot, and retied the ropes on Ms. Patterson. Kevin insisted he stuff rags into everybody's mouths. Then Kevin tied Kyle up, talking as he did.

"You guys have really messed me up, you know. I could have kept this up another month and then I would have been all set."

"I don't get it," Kyle said, hoping to distract Kevin from doing a good job on the ropes — and get a few answers. "How'd you make this thing work . . . and why?"

"The UFO was dad's idea. He put it together and he flies it most of the time. Not bad, huh? You'd never think to look at him that he used to be an engineer. Too bad he never could keep those jobs. We had money in those days. Dad kept getting fired because he didn't take no guff from nobody. And neither do I," Kevin added, yanking the rope around Kyle's wrists as tight as he could.

"How does it work?" Kyle asked.

"Dad bought one of those model airplane kits and modified it. He thought more people would come stay at this dump if there was something exciting going on here. And you know, the old geezer was right. We haven't had this many campers in the last five years, even though he jacked up the price to stay here."

"There's nothing illegal about doing that. Why tie all of us up?"

Kevin looped the last bit of rope around Kyle's ankles, checked the ropes on the others, and then walked back to the pile of stuff lying by the side of the cave. Kyle gave a start as he recognized the cooler that Mr. Burnidge had brought. Kevin noticed Kyle's look and smirked at him.

"Oh, I made my own little contribution to the plan. I added the little touch about robbing people's campsites while they were out staring at the dumb thing. Great way to stock the company store, wouldn't you say? You know," he said with a laugh, "you guys almost caught me the night it rained. Dad was planning to fly the saucer that night and I saw you all head out, so I raided your van. But the stupid model doesn't work good in the rain, so Dad had to put it down up by the cabin on the bluff and I almost didn't get out of your campsite in time. You guys were so dumb you didn't even see me running down the road with your cooler."

Kevin shook his head at their stupidity and reached down to grab a bag from the pile and opened it. "You didn't have much worth taking," he said contemptuously, "but lots of people did. Look at all this beautiful cash I found." He pulled a wad of bills several inches thick out of the bag and waved it in Kyle's face. "I was going to wait until I had like five thousand dollars, but I can't because of you snoopy noses. Still this'll get me pretty far. You know, it's amazing what people will leave laying around a tent. That's where this baby was, just laying around." He gestured toward the gun, which he had set down, carefully out of reach, while tying up Kyle. "The guy who lost it didn't even have the guts to tell the cops it was gone. It's not registered. Now if you don't mind, I'm out of here. Oh, and don't worry. My dad will find you — eventually. I wonder if he'll miss me as little as I'll miss him. California here I come."

Kevin stuffed the money back in the bag, picked up his gun, and sauntered out into the sunshine.

All four of the captives promptly began wiggling about, attempting to free themselves from the ropes. It hurt to roll around on the uneven ground, but there wasn't much choice if they were going to get themselves free. Karen scraped her arm on a rock and felt it start to bleed, but she just started rubbing the ropes around her wrists against the rock, hoping it was sharp enough to cut through them. Patrick managed to spit out the rag in his mouth, but he didn't dare shout until he was sure Kevin was gone. Kyle struggled in frustration trying just to loosen his bonds, but Kevin had made sure they were as tight as he could make them. Ms. Patterson wriggled around too, but she didn't have any more luck than the three detectives.

Karen felt tears start into her eyes, but then suddenly she heard voices outside the cave.

"Hey, Kevin, we had to come looking for you, man. You said you'd be down by the bridge twenty minutes ago."

"Big deal. Well, come on. We can go now."

"Hey, dude, look at this. There's a cave here."

"Awesome. Let's check it out."

"Don't go in there!" the four captives heard Kevin say sharply, but it was too late. The two young men with bald heads walked into the cave.

"Far out!" said the first as he sighted the UFO.

The second turned back to the entrance to say something to Kevin and saw him standing there pointing the gun. The young man shook his head sadly, "Not cool, dude."

"Now I'm going to have to tie the both of you up too," Kevin said, his voice angry and frustrated.

"I don't think that will be necessary," said yet another voice. Jonathan stood behind Kevin. He calmly reached over and pulled the gun from Kevin's hand.

"What is this place? Grand Central Station?" Kevin sank to the ground, more disgusted than anything else, and refused to say another word.

*   *   *   *   *   *   *   *   *   *   *

Surprisingly Kevin offered no resistance. Like many other bullies, he folded when he didn't have a clear advantage. He kept muttering under his breath about how unfair everything was, but he didn't even try to run away. Jonathan and the two young men untied everyone, and they all drove back to the camp office in Mr. Burnidge's van. Mr. Turner tried to bribe them all into not calling the police, but Jonathan refused to listen.

"I've been there," he said. "I spent a year in jail for theft, because I had to learn things the hard way. You aren't helping him by protecting him from the consequences of his actions. At his age he probably won't spend any time in jail, and this just might shock him into realizing how serious his choices are. If he gets away with this, he'll just do something like it again."

The police agreed with Jonathan and took Kevin and his dad down to police headquarters. Then everybody, including Ms. Patterson and the two young men, headed back to the campsite to fill Mr. Burnidge and Melanie in on what had happened.

"I don't get it," Karen said to Ms. Patterson, after they'd told Mr. Burnidge and Melanie their part of the story. "What was in this for you? Why did you keep looking for the UFO when your story had already run?"

"That wasn't the story I wanted — some little bit

lost on page four. You write a sensational UFO story and it gets picked up by the wire service. This was my chance to make it into the big time." Ms. Patterson sounded wistful rather than angry.

"How'd Mr. Chandler fit into this?" Kyle asked.

"Mike? How did you know about him?" asked Ms. Patterson.

Kyle blushed and confessed to overhearing their quarrel.

"Oh. Well, I guess that doesn't matter now. Mike's my fiance. And he's the science teacher at Preston High. I asked him to use part of his vacation to help me find out about the UFO because he knows so much about what it would take to make and fly something like this. He invents things all the time, like that fishing rod. We pretended not to know each other because we didn't want to tip anybody off that we were both investigating the UFO. That's why he took that strip that fell off the UFO from you. He was pretty sure Mr. Turner was behind the UFO and wanted to see if he'd give himself away if someone confronted him with a piece of it."

"But I saw it in the cave," said Patrick.

"Well, Mr. Turner wasn't in his office when Mike tried to see him, so I took it to get it analyzed — you know, just in case it was from outer space. I had it with me the day Kevin hit me on the head. He hit

126

me because I was getting too close to the cave and he thought that would scare me away. But when I woke up and saw the strip had been taken, I was just that much more convinced that I was on the right track."

"Well, you may not have a classic UFO story here, but I bet it makes a good story anyway," Patrick pointed out.

Ms. Patterson smiled. "Yeah," she said slowly, "it sure will."

Karen turned to Jonathan. "How'd you know where to look for us?"

"I wasn't looking for you. I was following them." He pointed to the two bald young men. "For some reason, I thought they were behind the UFO, so I was keeping an eye on them."

"Us!" The two young men thought that was hilariously funny.

"Yeah," Jonathan continued, shaking his head. "I didn't worry about you kids scouting along the river there as long as I knew they weren't there."

"Why were you two looking for Kevin?" Patrick asked.

"He was supposed to drive us upriver so we could take another canoe ride," one of the young men said. They seemed to think that was funny too.

"By the way," Mr. Burnidge said. "Your pictures

came back." He pointed to three envelopes lying on the picnic table. Karen, Kyle, and Patrick rushed over and grabbed them.

"Hey, these are pretty good," Kyle said.

"The UFO looks better on film than it did in real life," said Karen.

Everyone else crowded round to see the pictures. The circle of red and white lights did look pretty mysterious. Ms. Patterson asked if she could use one of the pictures in her new article and the three detectives agreed.

"Well, I guess that's another mystery solved," said Kyle with satisfaction.

"Courtesy of The Red Door Detective Club," Karen added, sending Patrick a wink.

"Yeah," agreed Patrick.

Kyle opened his mouth to protest, but Karen interrupted, "And we still have two days left here."

"And then two more weeks of summer vacation," Kyle said.

"But then school." Patrick groaned.

"Well, that's not so bad," Karen said. "I'm kind of looking forward to going back. I miss seeing all my friends."

"Yeah," Kyle agreed, "And besides, you never know what might happen in school. Maybe we'll find another mystery to solve."